Best w...
this special day
26th June '94,

Oriel

SAINTS

SAINTS

Frank Longford

HUTCHINSON

LONDON MELBOURNE AUCKLAND JOHANNESBURG

This edition first published in 1987 by Hutchinson, an imprint of
Century Hutchinson Ltd, Brookmount House, 62–65 Chandos Place,
London WC2N 4NW

Century Hutchinson Australia Pty Ltd
PO Box 496, 16-22 Church Street, Hawthorn, Victoria 3122, Australia

Century Hutchinson New Zealand Limited
PO Box 40–086, Glenfield, Auckland 10, New Zealand

Century Hutchinson South Africa (Pty) Ltd
PO Box 337, Berglvei, 2012 South Africa

British Library Cataloguing in Publication Data
Longford, Frank Pakenham, *Earl of*
　　Saints
　　1. Christian saints—Biography
　　I. Title
　　270　　　　BR1710

　　ISBN 0–09–171130–4

Photoset by Deltatype, Ellesmere Port, Cheshire
Printed and bound in Great Britain by
Anchor Brendon Ltd, Tiptree, Essex

CONTENTS

for Elizabeth

ACKNOWLEDGEMENTS

Many people have helped me in putting this book together – I can only thank them collectively, but there are a few names I cannot omit: Monsignor Stark in the first place; Philip Caraman, SJ; and Basil Rooke-Ley.

I
INTRODUCTION

'The question: What is a saint?' wrote Jacques Douillet (*What is a Saint?* 1958), could, in one sense, be answered in this way: 'A saint is a person now dead whom the Catholic Church allows to be publicly venerated.' That is bound to be our starting point. The bulk of this book will be devoted to a selected eighteen saints who have been canonised by the Catholic Church. Two Orthodox saints are added. I am aware that other Churches have their own methods of singling out those whom they regard as specially holy.

Besides the twenty saints I include several other short essays as well as a concluding chapter. I deal with three great Christians: Martin Luther, John Henry Newman and William Temple; with six of the martyrs of the twentieth century commemorated in Canterbury Cathedral; and with the views of four outstanding modern writers on sanctity, as expressed in some of the characters in their books.

This Introduction offers a few remarks about Anglican and Orthodox ideas of sanctity. I was troubled by the question of whether or not to deal with holy men outside Christianity. I had drawn up essays on Mohammed and Gandhi, and was preparing one on Maimonides, but came to the conclusion that if I proceeded further along that line the book would lose its balance.

The oldest writings in Christian literature are Saint Paul's letters. The one which he wrote to his friends at Philippi in Macedonia begins: 'Paul and Timothy, the servants of Jesus Christ, to all the saints in Christ Jesus that are in Philippi. . .'. The letter ends: 'Greet all the saints in Christ Jesus'. Evidently for Paul the saints were all the faithful. Paul was a Jew of the Jews. His idea of holiness would have been carried over from the Old Testament. God himself, supremely holy, had decided to sanctify, that is to render holy, the Hebrew people. But it needed the incarnation of the Word, it needed Christ to make this idea of holiness possible and actual. The human nature of all mankind, not just the Jews, was sanctified in Jesus.

In principle, it can be hoped that all will be saved. It is right, therefore, that they should be called saints, as St Paul does call them. But (to quote Douillet again): 'actual usage now reserves the title of saint to those who march in front and provide an example to the Christian people. To those whose lives give proof of unquestionable holiness'.

In 1983, Pope John Paul II issued new laws for the causes of the saints. His accompanying statement brings us up to date with the official Catholic standards. 'At various times,' he wrote, 'God chooses from among these many who, having followed more closely the example of Christ, give outstanding testimony to the kingdom of Heaven by shedding their blood, or by an heroically virtuous life.'

From the earliest beginnings of Christianity, 'the Church, which has always believed that the apostles and martyrs were quite closely joined to us in Christ, has shown them, together with the Blessed Virgin Mary and the angels, particular veneration. It has devoutly implored their intercession. To these were soon added others who had imitated closely the chastity and poverty of Christ and, finally, others 'whose outstanding practice of the Christian virtues and the divine charisma recommend them to the pious devotion and imitation of the faithful.'

When a man (or woman) is canonised, he is deemed to have attained paradise; in other words, to be in Heaven. He has attained this state at the time of canonisation, which does not rule out the possibility, or even likelihood, of his having spent some period in purgatory after death. It is now held by the Church to be safe to pray to him.

The procedure today is very elaborate, but under the new laws referred to above, not quite so elaborate as it was. In June 1986 Cardinal Newman's 'cause' was referred to Rome by the Birmingham diocese, supported by the entire hierarchy of England and Wales.

The attempts to secure the canonisation of Newman (see Chapter 19) have taken many years to come to fruition. The formal opening of the cause did not take place until 1958, and many years of toil followed. In Newman's case, his enormous literary output presented an obstacle. Today, however, the burden of reading and producing every single word he wrote has been much lightened.

In the beginning it was the martyrs who were venerated. The faithful had been present at a martyr's trial and execution, and could see for themselves that he or she had stoutly professed Christ and had been put to death for his or her fidelity. Those who confessed Christ at the peril of their lives were looked on as martyrs, on the same footing as those who had shed their blood. These and other survivors were not martyrs but confessors and they took a high place in their Church. As persecution lessened, the ascetics began to succeed the martyrs as heroes of the faith. St Anthony and St Simeon, for example, were treated with enormous respect. Bishops who were known for their influential activity and their writings, such as St Ambrose at Milan, or for their austere life or apostolic works, such as St Martin at Tours, were at first commemorated on a different basis: martyrs were invoked, bishops were prayed for, but gradually the honours given to ascetics were accorded to bishops, so that they in their turn became regarded as confessors.

In the earlier centuries no special procedure was considered necessary. A system developed under which a bishop would give his approval to spontaneous recognition, or occasionally withhold it. Rome did not at first lay claim to a control of canonisation. The oldest case we know comes from AD 993. The Bishop of Augsburg, during a synod presided over by Pope John XV, asked permission to read to the assembly an account of the life and miracles of his predecessor, Ulric. This done, the Pope declared, with the unanimous agreement of those present, that it was right and proper to venerate the memory of this holy bishop. That was, as yet in very summary form, the first recorded process of canonisation. It was Pope Alexander III (1159–81) who decided that, in future, causes of canonisation should be reserved for the Holy See. The procedure of canonisation at Rome was made more and more explicit until in 1634 Pope Urban VIII laid down the broad lines of the rules for approval as they are today. They reached a definitive formulation in the code of Canon Law of 1917. It should be noted that in 1634 thousands of canonisations that had taken place previously were not called in question. It is impossible, therefore, to say how many Catholic saints can be legitimately venerated.

Today, as is well known, the law provides for two stages in canonisation. After the first, the servant of God is declared Beatus

(Blessed). This authorisation is only provisional; nevertheless the title is not bestowed until after minute enquiries.

The second stage is canonisation, a definitive act. It is said by good authorities to be 'on the verge of Papal infallibility'. The general rule today is that one miracle must have come about through the intercession of the beatified man or woman, except for martyrs, and another one before canonisation can be approved. In 1935, however, Saint John Fisher and Saint Thomas More were canonised with dispensation from proof of miracles. It was the first example of this since the legislation of Urban VIII, but there is no reason to suppose that it will be the last.

On the whole question of miracles, Father Caraman, SJ, in his article 'Holiness in the Catholic Tradition', assures us: 'The regulations alter and are likely to be altered again. Since they are laid down by the Pope, the Pope can, in selected cases, dispense with them. Miracles worked by God through the intercession of the saints were not always a requirement for the canonisation of martyrs, and there have been both confessors and martyrs canonised in this century, without investigation into alleged miracles.' Caraman eloquently concludes: 'Whatever fate the world may suffer, the saints remain heroes, protectors, patrons, friends and intercessors; they are the honoured members of the Christian community, examples of virtue that all, by their baptism into Christ, are pledged to pursue; their task is not completed with their death, nor their power for good curtailed by it; they do not stand between the Christian and Christ.'

What is the Anglican approach to sanctity? I have studied with interest *Every Man's Book of Saints* by Brother Kenneth CGO. Roughly three-quarters of those included on an individual basis are saints canonised by the Catholic Church. The others include some truly noble figures, e.g. Julian of Norwich, Thomas Cranmer, George Herbert, Richard Hooker, John and Charles Wesley, William Wilberforce and Josephine Butler. There are also group commemorations which mention contemporary personalities like Dietrich Bonhoeffer and William Temple. These groups are placed under the heading 'Saints and Martyrs' (not simply 'Saints'). A chapel at Canterbury commemorates twelve martyrs of the present century.

Whatever may be the case with individual Anglicans, their Church does not officially recognise the invocation of individual saints in prayer, or allocate to them any special status, such as that of being already in Heaven. The Liturgical Commission in the sixties and seventies proposed a revised list of 'lesser festivals and commemorations'. The Virgin Mary and the Apostles are additional and in a sense more elevated. The Commission had this to say about what they called 'the second list': 'It gave expression to our belief that sanctity is not confined to the ages before the fourteenth century, and that the names of holy men and women of more recent times ought to be included in the calendar, so that it may reflect the variety of Christian witness and holiness up to our own times.' The Liturgical Commission admitted: 'Objective criteria by which to decide which persons should be included and which should not are difficult to determine, and even more difficult to apply.'

They conclude this section of their report: 'Our list may seem subjective, and we think that this is inevitable. We have therefore been careful to provide that dioceses should be free to add other names for diocesan and local commemoration, and in doing so they would be taking the first step to secure their ultimate addition to the general calendar. The Group Commemorations of the Saints and Martyrs of the five continents provide a further opportunity to introduce the names of individuals. To them we have added the Saints and Martyrs of the Reformation Era on October 31. We believe that this will provide an opportunity to commemorate those who were loyal to their beliefs on both sides of the Reformation controversy.'

It has been emphasised to me that the Anglican list is essentially representative, not exhaustive. There is no reason to assume that someone included is held to be holier than someone excluded. The Catholic Church, for its part, has never denied that there have been large numbers of men and women who were suitable for canonisation, but who were not in fact canonised.

The Orthodox tradition of sanctity is closer to the Roman Catholic than the Anglican tradition or that of any other reformed Churches. A learned authority, Dr Paul Evdokimov, has written in a contribution to the symposium 'Man's Concern with Holiness' that, in the Orthodox Church, 'the veneration of the saints is rooted in the Communion of Saints . . . In the risen Christ the natural intercession of the living for the living finds this same

entire freedom, leading on to the equally natural intercession of
the saints, which is their manner of participating, in heaven, in the
destiny of the Church on earth. We are surrounded by the
protecting prayers of the saints.'

The Orthodox Church, like the Roman, but unlike the Anglican
Church and the other reformed Churches, officially selects a
number of much admired personalities and canonises them:
Nectarius, Patriarch of Jerusalem (*d.* 1680), formulated the three
conditions necessary for canonisation:

1 Unquestionable orthodoxy of faith;
2 Holiness of life, and a confession of faith which would go as far as
  martyrdom if necessary;
3 Obvious manifestations of divine grace during lifetime or after
  death: miracles, healings, spiritual help, often but not always
  physical incorruptibility.

In the Orthodox Church, however, there are no precise rules or
legal formalities to determine the procedure of canonisation. In
the words of Dr Evdokimov: 'It is something which evades all set
rulings. The Church glorifies different categories of saints:
patriarchs, prophets, martyrs, workers of miracles, theologians
and Fathers of the Church, monks, ascetics, spiritual fathers,
princes, doctors and pious laymen.'

The Orthodox Church, again like the Catholic but unlike the
Anglican Church, attaches the prefix 'St' to its selected notables.
It would be as unthinkable not to refer to 'Saint Serafim' of Sarov
(1759–1793) as it would be to refer to 'Saint' William Temple, a
man of God to whom I have tried to pay tribute.

In my concluding chapter, I have dealt briefly with the question
of how many of our selected saints could be described as mystics.
It is obviously a question on which it would be distinctly
ridiculous to dogmatise. But in advance of our discussion of
individual saints, it seems appropriate to say a few words about
mysticism in relation to sanctity.

Definitions of mysticism abound. Some would demand of the
mystic that he has achieved to a greater or lesser extent union with
God. A slightly less stringent test is applied by F. C. Happold in
his well-known book, *Mysticism*. 'In the religious mystic,' he
writes, 'there is a direct experience of the Presence of God.'
Mysticism in a broad sense is discovered in all the main religions.

From the Christian point of view a direct experience of Jesus Christ is surely required. But mystics are not automatically saints, or saints mystics. Mystics as such have not been canonised, though no doubt the Catholic Church has taken into account their mystical experiences in assessing their sanctity. On the other hand thousands of saints have been accepted as such without mysticism coming into it one way or the other. The two concepts, mysticism and sanctity, overlap but they are essentially distinguishable.

Part I
TWENTY SAINTS

2
ST PETER
AD 64

St Peter is the only apostle among our selected saints and the only one of them who knew Jesus Christ when he was on earth. St Peter stands therefore on a different footing from the others. For much of his life we have the excellent evidence of the Gospels and the first part of the Acts, to which I would personally add, though the matter has been disputed, the two epistles which bear St Peter's name. Roman Catholics have a special attitude of reverence towards St Peter, in their eyes the founder of the Christian Church. It is significant to quote the witness of Dr Lowe, Anglican Dean of Christ Church: 'No one,' wrote Dr Lowe, 'can take from St Peter his special distinction as the leading disciple of Jesus, the first witness of the resurrection, the first head of the Church, the rock in a special sense on which it was built.' Roman Catholics, though not Dr Lowe, are convinced that the commission given to Peter initiated an apostolic succession which expresses itself today in Pope John Paul II.

However, I do not feel it necessary to pursue here the claims of Peter's successors. St Peter himself will keep us busy enough. Again, the origins of St Peter are not important for our purpose. It would seem that he was born in Bethesda in Galilee, an area of mixed populations, where some Greek would have been spoken. He seems initially to have borne both a Hebrew and a Greek name, Symeon and Simon. At the time of his 'call' by Christ he was married and lived in a house at Capernaum with his brother Andrew and his mother-in-law. His occupation was that of a fisherman. Luke says that he was in partnership with James and John. 'He was in the fishing business, not as proprietor or director of a big concern, nor yet as a mere labourer, but as a son of a man who had his own small boat and who, though operating in quite a small way, could afford to hire a group of assistants' (Lowe).

The account of St Peter's call is not quite the same in the

Synoptics and St John. It is more vivid in the latter: 'The next day again John stood and two of his disciples, and beholding Jesus walking, he saith: Behold the Lamb of God. And the two disciples heard him speak, and they followed Jesus. And Jesus turning and seeing them following him saith to them: What seek you? Who said to him: Rabbi (which is to say, being interpreted, Master) where dwellest thou? He saith to them, come and see. They came and saw where he abode, and they stayed with him that day. And Andrew, the brother of Simon Peter, was one of the two who had heard of John and followed him.'

Andrew said to Peter: 'We have found the Messiah, which is being interpreted the Christ.' Next day he brought him to Jesus. Mother Mary Simeon in her book *Simon Called Peter* described what followed as 'the most historic meeting which the world has ever seen. The meeting between Christ, the Son of God and his first Vicar upon earth.' Jesus, looking on him, said: 'Thou are Simon the son of Jonah – thou shalt be called Sephas which is interpreted Peter.' In Aramaic the Greek word *petra* or *petros* means stone or rock. I have already quoted Dr Lowe as treating Peter as 'the rock in a special sense on which the Church was to be built'.

Peter is mentioned many times in the Gospels and always first in any list of apostles. What kind of person do they show him to be? It is only possible here to deal with four episodes, the second and third going closely together.

Jesus had obliged his disciples, after the feeding of the five thousand, 'to go up into the boat and to go before him over the water'. The boat was tossed by the waves, the wind was contrary. In the fourth watch of the night he came to them, walking on the sea. The apostles, supposing it to be an apparition, cried out in alarm. Jesus said: 'Be of good heart, it is I. Fear ye not,' at which Peter sprang forward, every nerve aflame. 'Lord,' he cried, 'if it be you, bid me come to you upon the waters.' Jesus replied with the monosyllable: 'Come.' 'And Peter going down out of the boat walked upon the water. For a few moments the miracle was performed.' Peter had faith, but not quite sufficient faith. 'Seeing the wind strong', he was afraid. He began to sink and he cried out, desperately this time: 'Lord, save me.' Jesus immediately stretched out his hand and took hold of him, saying to him sadly, but no doubt understandingly: 'Oh, you of little faith, why did you doubt?' Jesus and Peter made their way back to the boat, the wind ceased; those who were in the boat, we are told, adored Jesus, saying: 'Indeed you are the Son of God.' Peter had shown himself so ardent, but so easily deflected from a noble purpose by a limitation of faith.

The historic passage from Matthew xvi must be given in full.

13 Jesus went to the territory near the town of Caesarea Philippi, where he asked his disciples: 'Who do people say the Son of Man is?'

14 'Some say John the Baptist,' they answered. 'Others say Elijah, while others say Jeremiah or some other prophet.'

15 'What about you?' he asked them. 'Who do you say I am?'

16 Simon Peter answered: 'You are the Messiah, the Son of the living God.'

Peter had risen gloriously to the occasion and he received in return the greatest conceivable accolade: 'Blessed are you,' said Jesus, 'Simon bar Jonah, because flesh and blood have not revealed it to you, but my Father who is in Heaven . . . and I will give you the key to the kingdom of Heaven and whatsoever you bind on earth shall be bound also in Heaven, and whatsoever you loose on earth shall be loosed also in Heaven.'

Peter was lifted up to the heights and in the next moment he was cast to the depths. Jesus told his disciples starkly that he must go to Jerusalem and suffer much from the Elders, the Chief Priest and the teachers of the law. He must be put to death, but three days later he would be raised to life. 'Peter took him aside and began to rebuke him: "God forbid it, Lord," he said, "that must never happen to you."' Jesus turned around and said to Peter, in the most terrible words that could be used to any man, whether or not a disciple: 'Get you behind me, Satan. You are an obstacle in my way, because these thoughts of yours don't come from God but from man.'

But within six days, possibly less, Peter had been forgiven. Jesus took with him Peter and James and John, and led them up a high mountain where they were alone. 'As they looked on, a change came over Jesus: his face was shining like the sun, and his clothes were dazzling white. Then the three disciples saw Moses and Elijah talking with Jesus. So Peter spoke up and said to Jesus: "Lord, how good it is that we are here! If you wish, I will make three tents here, one for you, one for Moses and one for Elijah."

While he was talking, a shining cloud came over them, and a voice from the cloud said: "This is my own dear Son, with whom I am pleased – listen to him!" ' Once again, Peter, beyond all question the leader of the apostles, was totally loyal, full of the desire to worship in the right way, but still far from comprehending the spiritual forces into which he was being rapidly absorbed.

And so, passing over many other mentions of Peter, we come to the Passion. Once again certain particular episodes are telling. At the last supper, Jesus rose and 'laying aside his garments and having taken a towel, girded himself. After that he put water into a basin and began to wash the feet of the disciples and to wipe them with the towel wherewith he was girded. He comes therefore to Simon Peter. And Peter said to him: "Lord, do you wash my feet?" '

Peter's humility strikes us as commendable, but Jesus had a deeper message to impart. 'If I wash you not, you will have no part with me,' a restatement of a message conveyed in so many different ways: 'The Son of Man has come not to be served but to serve others.'

One other outburst of Peter's during the supper must be recounted. Jesus had said: 'Whither I go, you cannot come.' Peter replied: 'Why cannot I follow you now? I will lay down my life for thee.' Jesus said: 'Will you lay down your life for me? I say to you, Peter, today, even in this night before the cock crow twice, you will deny me thrice.'

In the Garden of Gethsemane, Jesus, after agonising in prayer, returned three times to Peter, James and John, and each time found them asleep. He told Peter, gently you may be sure: 'What, could you not watch with me one hour? Watch and pray that you enter not into temptation. The spirit indeed is willing, but the flesh is weak.' When the arresting party arrived Simon Peter, acting on a far from ignoble impulse, 'having a sword, drew it, and striking the servant of the High Priest cut off his ear.'

When Jesus was carried off, all the disciples fled. But Peter 'followed afar off even to the court of the High Priest and, going in, he sat with the servants that he might see the end.' His never-to-be-forgotten denials followed. On the third occasion, after a little while, the men standing there came to Peter: 'Of course you are one of them,' they said. 'After all, the way you speak gives you away!' Then Peter said: 'I swear that I am telling the truth!

May God punish me if I am not! I do not know that man!' Just then the cock crowed for the second time. Jesus turned and looked into Peter's eyes. One cannot doubt that he conveyed a message all the more distressing because it was one of unbroken love. Peter remembered the word of the Lord, as he had said: 'Before the cock crow twice, you will three times deny me.' Peter stumbled away into the darkness.

We do not meet Peter again till Easter morning. His primacy is as evident as ever. 'Be not affrighted,' said the angel at the sepulchre to the holy women, 'you seek Jesus of Nazareth who was crucified; he is risen; he is not here; behold the place where they laid him, but go and tell his disciples and *Peter* that he goeth before you into Galilee. There you shall see him as he told you.' Jesus appeared to the apostles that evening and a week later in Jerusalem. Peter of course would have been present, but excluding a traditional appearance to the Virgin Mary it would seem that the very first appearance was to him.

When the two men of Emmaus, who had encountered Christ on their walk, broke in on the eleven disciples in Jerusalem, they were told: 'The Lord is risen indeed. He has appeared to Simon.' In Corinthians iv, St Paul writes: 'Christ died for our sins, as written in the scriptures. He was raised to life three days later, as written in the scriptures. He appeared to *Peter* and then to all twelve apostles.'

But a more explicit account yet comes down to us of how Jesus showed himself to the disciples at the Sea of Tiberius: 'There were together Simon Peter and Thomas, who is called Didymus and Nathaniel, who was of Cana of Galilee, and the sons of Zebedee and two others of the disciples. Simon Peter saith to them: "I go a-fishing;" they say to him: "we also come with you." And they went forth and entered into the ship and that night they caught nothing. In the morning Jesus stood on the shore. He said to them: "Cast the net on the right side of the ship and you shall find." They cast therefore on the right side of the ship, and now they were not able to draw the multitude of fishes.'

Peter as always was desperately ready to act. 'The disciple whom Jesus loves said to him: "It is the Lord." ' Peter plunges immediately into the sea for no reason except the desire once again to be close to his master. The others were left to bring the boat ashore. It was Peter, however, who went up and drew the net to land, 'full of great fishes, one hundred and fifty-three.'

After they had finished the meal, Jesus said to Simon Peter: 'Simon, son of John, do you love me more than these?' Peter replied: 'Yes, Lord, you know that I love you.' Jesus then said: 'Feed my lambs.' Then, later, a third time: 'Simon, son of John, do you love me?' Peter was grieved because he was asked this same question a third time, and replied: 'Lord, you know all things, you know that I love you.' At which point Christ said: 'Feed my sheep.'

Christ was conveying to Peter in the most emphatic manner a message of unlimited forgiveness and laying on him an equally unlimited responsibility. The last words that he used to him after Peter had asked about the future of the disciples whom Jesus loved were: 'So I will have him remain until I come. What is it to you? Follow you me.'

During the life of Christ, Peter had come to stand out as the solemn shepherd of the flock. After the crucifixion, he took the lead as of right. Upon his initiative, measures were taken to fill up the missing place caused by the defection of Judas Iscariot. The interpretation of the experience of Pentecost was undertaken by Peter 'standing up with the eleven'. In a loud voice he began to speak to the crowd: 'Fellow Jews and all of you who live in Jerusalem, listen to me and let me tell you what this means. These people are not drunk as you suppose – it is only nine o'clock in the morning.' Having quoted the prophet Joel, he proceeded to deliver the first classic statement of the Christian faith: 'Jesus of Nazareth was a man whose divine authority was clearly proven to you by all the miracles and wonders which God performed through him. . . . You killed him by letting sinful men crucify him. But God raised him from death, because it was impossible that death should hold him prisoner.'

After quoting David, he concluded: 'All the people of Israel then are to know for sure that this Jesus, whom you crucified, God has made Lord and Messiah.' The people, deeply troubled, pleaded with Peter to tell them what they could do to be saved. Peter left them in no doubt. 'Each one of you must turn away from his sins and be baptised in the name of Jesus Christ, so that your sins will be forgiven you; and you will receive God's gift of the Holy Spirit.' This message in essentials he was to repeat in later addresses.

In his dealings with the Sanhedrin, Peter was treated as the leader of the community. We are told that 'as Peter came by, the sick were disposed in the streets, so that at least his shadow might over-shadow some of them.' Besides presiding at Jerusalem, Peter also travelled, visiting the believers and evangelising at Lydda, Joppa and Caesaraea. In Caesaraea, he converted and baptised the Gentile centurion Cornelius and his companion. Peter was the first to treat Gentiles as admissible to the Church.

Later, he appears to have faltered in this respect, and been rebuked by St Paul. He humbly recognised his mistake. Somewhere between AD 41 and AD 44, he was imprisoned by Herod. On his release, he departed from Jerusalem to another place. He was to live until AD 64, but for whatever reason he disappears from the Acts. We must rely therefore on sometimes inconsistent traditions for the last twenty years of his life. There seems no doubt that he was continuously engaged in missionary work over a wide area. He is reported to have returned to Jerusalem only once. He certainly went to Antioch and may have founded a church there. It is likely that he worked for a time in Corinth. An overwhelming tradition (which I accept) treats him as having died a martyr's death in Rome.

Roman Catholic tradition associates him with Rome far more closely. It is sometimes claimed that he spent as much as twenty-five years there, though exiled for some years before returning to Rome in AD 56. Pope Pius XII, in his Christmas message of 1950, distinguished a small area under St Peter's as his burial place.

There is a strong tradition about Peter's death, which I would like to accept. As it was believed that Nero was meditating a violent persecution, the Christians of Rome begged St Peter to conceal himself. As he left the city he was met by Jesus. Asked by St Peter where he was going, Jesus replied: 'I am going to Rome to be crucified again.' St Peter immediately retraced his steps to be imprisoned, tortured and finally put to death. He asked his executioner that he might be crucified with his head downwards, deeming himself unworthy to be placed in the same position on the cross as his master had been.

One cannot omit all mention of the two letters from St Peter. The first was addressed to Christians scattered through the northern part of Asia Minor. The main purpose of the letter was to encourage the readers who were facing persecution and suffering for their faith. One sentence read: 'My dear friends, do not be surprised at the painful test you are suffering, as though something unusual were happening to you. Rather be glad that you are sharing Christ's sufferings, so that you may be full of joy when his glory is revealed.'

The second letter was addressed to a wide circle of early Christians. His main concern was to combat the work of false teachers and the immorality which resulted from such teaching. There is clear assurance of the second coming: 'We wait for what God has promised, new heavens and a new earth, where righteousness will be at home.'

What was Peter like? There have been many pious speculations about his appearance. He is presented as a much bigger man, for instance, than St Paul, with whom he is deemed to have worked in Rome. Certain qualities stand out unambiguously from the printed page. Clearly he was impetuous and daring; quick to speak, quick to promise, yet flawed with a certain instability. There was in him a moral resilience which enabled him to pull himself up off the floor and prove his courage at the end. We are entitled to suppose that he was a man who overcame his frailties to achieve heroic virtue. We can identify all too easily with his weaknesses and aspire to acquire his strength; partly for that reason he will always occupy a special place in human hearts.

Why did Christ select Peter to be the leader of his Church? We shall never know. But I see him as a man who has never been excelled in the ardour of his soul.

3
THE EARLY MARTYRS
ST IGNATIUS OF ANTIOCH AD 35–C107
ST POLYCARP AD C79–C155
ST PERPETUA AD C203
ST FELICITY AD C203

St Peter died in agony for the sake of his faith, an experience that marked out the earliest saints of the Catholic Church, who were martyrs. There were a large number of these during the Ten Classical Persecutions before the 'peace of the Church' – the recognition of Christianity by the Emperor Constantine by AD 313. Here we can touch on only three of them: St Ignatius of Antioch, St Polycarp of Smyrna and St Perpetua, with whom is usually joined the slave girl St Felicity.

St Ignatius, born about AD 35, and Bishop of Antioch, was arrested in AD 107 and taken away to be martyred in Rome. On the way he received visitors from several churches and wrote a number of letters which conveyed the flavour of a remarkable spirituality.

His total commitment and joy in martyrdom are evident in his letter to the Ephesians. He expressed his hope of obtaining their prayers for the privilege of fighting with beasts at Rome: 'By so doing, I might be enabled to be a true disciple.' His message is illustrated in the following passage: 'Be yourselves gentle in answer to their wrath; be humble-minded in answer to their proud-speaking; offer prayer for their blasphemy; be steadfast in the faith for their error; be gentle for their cruelty, and do not seek to retaliate. Let us be proved their brothers by our gentleness and let us be imitators of the Lord, and seek who may suffer the more wrong, be the more destitute, the more despised; that no plant of the devil be found in you, but that you may remain in all purity and sobriety in Jesus Christ, both in the flesh and in the spirit.'

His insistence on being allowed to undergo horrendous suffering is vehemently expressed in his letter to the Romans: 'I am afraid,' he tells his friends, 'of your love, lest even that do me wrong. For it is easy for you to do what you will, but it is difficult for me to attain to God if you do not spare me.' That is, if they do not stop trying to rescue him. He makes the same point again and again. 'If you are silent concerning me, I am a word of God, but if you love my flesh, I shall again be only a cry.'

ὁ ἐμὸς ἔρως ἐσταύρωται.

Michael Burghers   delineavit et sculpsit.

He by no means takes it for granted that he will die heroically. For this purpose he begs them for their prayers: 'Only pray for me for strength, both inward and outward, that I may not merely speak, but also have the will, that I may not only be called a Christian, but may also be found to be one. For if I be found to be one, I can also be called one, and then be deemed faithful when I no longer am visible in the world.'

Then followed the unforgettable passage: 'I am dying willingly for God's sake, if you do not hinder it. I beseech you, be not "an unseasonable kindness to me." Suffer me to be eaten by the beasts, through whom I can attain to God. I am God's wheat, and I am ground by the teeth of wild beasts that I may be found pure bread of Christ.'

For St Ignatius, as for so many other martyrs, a death for the sake of Christ, and in the style of Christ, was the crown and goal of Christian living. I feel that it is this which is recognised above all in his being acknowledged a saint.

The last of St Ignatius's letters was written to the future St Polycarp. Born about AD 79, Polycarp was, by the time of St Ignatius's martyrdom (AD 107), already Bishop of Smyrna, though still under thirty years of age. He in his turn, now aged eighty-six, was arrested in AD 155 and brought to martyrdom. The contemporary account by Marcian is exceptionally full and vivid. When his arrest seemed imminent, he fell into a trance while praying. He saw the pillow under his head burning with fire and he turned and said to those who were with him: 'I must be burnt alive.'

When the arresting party arrived, he ordered food and drink to be set before them 'whatever they should wish', and he asked them to give him an hour to pray without hindrance. To this they assented, and he stood and prayed, filled with the grace of God, so that for two hours he could not be silent. Those who listened were astonished and many repented that they had come against such a venerable old man. When he entered the arena there came a voice from heaven, heard, it would seem, only by his friends. 'Be strong Polycarp and play the man.' He hardly needed this last-minute instruction. When the Pro-consul pressed him and said: 'take the oath (to swear by the genius of Caesar) and I'll let you go. Otherwise revile Christ,' Polycarp replied: 'Eighty-and-six years have I been His servant, and He has done me no wrong! How can I blaspheme my King who saved me?'

The Pro-consul threatened him with wild beasts. Polycarp replied: 'Call to them. For repentance from better to worse is not allowed us; it is good to change from evil to righteousness.' The Pro-consul became more and more hostile. 'I will cause you to be consumed by fire, if you despise the beasts, unless you repent.' But Polycarp said: 'You threaten with the fire that burns for a time and is quickly quenched, for you do not know the fire which awaits the wicked in the judgement to come and in everlasting punishment. But why are you waiting? Come, do what you will.'

The attempt to burn Polycarp alive is described by eye-witnesses with obvious sincerity but, it will be thought today, with some poetic licence. So also would the last scene of all. 'At length, the lawless men, seeing that his body could not be consumed by the fire, demanded that the executioner should go up and stab him with the dagger. When he did this there came out a dove, and much blood, so that the fire was quenched. And all the crowd marvelled. There was so much difference between the unbelievers and the elect.' The emergence of a dove may be taken symbolically. Let us say that his glorious death stirred the imagination of his supporters so that the precise details of what occurred seemed – and seem today – unimportant.

The friends of Polycarp demanded his dead body. They were told that they were leaving the crucified one, Jesus Christ, and beginning to worship this man, Polycarp. They made the foreseeable answer: 'They do not know that we shall not ever be able either to abandon Christ, who suffered for the salvation of those who are being saved in the whole world, the innocent or sinners, or to worship any other. For him we worship as the Son of God, but the martyrs we love as disciples and imitators of the Lord; and rightly, because of their unsurpassable affection toward their own kind and teacher. God grant that we too may be their companions and fellow-disciples.'

The most poignant of all the martyrs' narratives is called the Passion of St Perpetua and St Felicity. It holds a unique place in Christian annals. During the fourth century it was publicly read in the churches of North Africa. It was so popular that St Augustine had to protest that it should not be put on a level with the books of the Bible. There were six martyrs in this group at Carthage on 7 March AD 203. They include Vibia Perpetua, twenty-two years old, a married woman of noble birth with a baby son, and Felicity, a pregnant slave girl. Perpetua was much troubled for the welfare of her baby who was with her, and by the entreaties of her aged father. He, unfortunately, was a pagan and could not understand his favourite child's resolution.

Perpetua's own account brings it before us all too easily. 'While,' says she, 'we were still with the persecutors, my father, for the sake of his affection for me, was persisting in seeking to turn me away and to cast me down from the faith. "Father," said I, "do you see, let us say, this vessel lying here to be a little pitcher, or something else?" And he said: "I see it to be so." And I replied to him: "Can it be called by any other name than what it is?" And he said: "No." "Neither can I call myself anything else than what I am, a Christian." Then my father, provoked at this saying, threw himself upon me as if he would tear my eyes out. But he only distressed me, and went away overcome by the Devil's arguments.'

At the trial all were condemned to the beasts. Perpetua's baby was taken from her, and he, 'as God willed, wanted no more to be suckled, nor did I take fever, that I might not be troubled by anxiety for the baby or by pain in my breasts.' During this period Perpetua had several dreams or visions, of which only one can be given here. She seemed to be in the arena confronted by an ugly Egyptian. The man of huge stature, gloriously clothed, told her she must fight with the Egyptian, and if she triumphed she would receive the branch that he carried, on which were golden apples. Perpetua was stripped and rubbed down with oil by attendants, and 'I became a man'. She fought with the Egyptian and overcame him. She received the branch, and the bearer of it kissed her, saying 'Peace be with you, daughter.' 'And I awoke, understanding that I should not fight with beasts but with the Devil. But I knew that victory was mine.'

Meanwhile, so the ancient account proceeds, Felicity, the slave girl, eight months' pregnant, was in great grief lest on account of her pregnancy she should be delayed, because pregnant women were not allowed to be publicly punished, and lest she should shed her sacred and guiltless blood among some who had been wicked subsequently.

Her prayers were granted. 'Immediately afterwards her pains came upon her and then, with the difficulty natural to an eight months' delivery, in the labour of bringing forth she was sorrowing, one of the prison servants said to her: "You who are in such suffering now, what will you do when you are thrown to the beasts, which you despised when you refused to sacrifice to the gods?" And she replied: "Now it is I that suffer what I suffer; but then there will be another in me, who will suffer for me, because I also am about to suffer for Him." Thus she brought forth a little girl which a certain sister brought up as her daughter.'

The narrative continues: 'The day of their victory shone forth and they proceeded from the prison into the amphitheatre as if to an assembly, joyous and of brilliant countenances; if perchance shrinking it was with joy, and not with fear. Perpetua followed with placid look, and with step and gait as a matron of Christ, beloved of God, casting down the lustre of her eyes from the gaze of all. Moreoever, Felicity was there, rejoicing that she had safely given birth, so that she might fight with the wild beasts; from the blood of the midwife to the blood of the gladiator, to wash after childbirth with a second baptism.'

For the young women a fierce cow was prepared. Stripped and clothed with nets, they were led forward. 'The populace shuddered as they saw one young woman of delicate frame and another with breasts still dripping from her recent childbirth.' Perpetua was tossed to the ground. She was concerned only to make sure that her torn garment covered her nakedness and that her dishevelled hair was dealt with in a fashion becoming to a martyr. She saw Felicity 'crushed' and helped her to her feet. The two women stood together 'till the brutality of the populace was appeased'. But there was no escape and indeed that was the last thing that any of the martyrs were looking for. Perpetua herself placed the wavering right hand of the gladiator at her throat. The recorder could not repress the reflection: 'Possibly such a woman would not have been slain unless she herself had willed it, because she was feared by the impure spirits.'

All the contemporary commentators insist that the martyrs commemorated provide glorious examples to help and strengthen their own and succeeding generations. When we read such stories as those of Perpetua and Felicity, it is not difficult to share their conviction. It may be felt by some people that the martyrs seemed to rush into suffering, not masochistically, but with what seemed often like foolhardiness. Was it more than bravery? Was there a spiritual dimension to their willingness to suffer? I do not myself feel any doubt about the answer.

An emphasis runs through all of them on God, Jesus Christ, the gathering of the brethren in the Church, indwelt corporately and individually by the Holy Spirit. The thoughts and lives of these Christians are permeated by the sacred Scriptures. In thirteen of these narratives there are over two hundred and fifty separate quotations from, or allusions to the text of the Bible, mostly of course the New Testament. There is no 'multiplicity', no complication, no hint of dissipation of spiritual energy.

Donald Attwater acknowledges that the recovery of such a primitive simplicity is impossible for most Christians in the late twentieth century. He suggests, however, that there is no reason why we should not strive for a special participation in the victory of Christ, such as the martyrs believed they enjoyed. This seems to me well said. I will suggest a further encouragement. In the last two thousand years there have been countless further examples of Christian nobility, high and low, if we know where to look for them. They are available to us as they were not to the early martyrs. Our task is not necessarily made harder because our outlook is so much more complicated than theirs.

4
ST AUGUSTINE OF HIPPO
354–430

No list of saints, however brief, is likely to leave out St Augustine of Hippo. No saint, unless it be St Paul, has left behind him a book so widely read as Augustine's *Confessions*. No saint's autobiography compares with it for popularity unless, in recent times, that of St Teresa of Lisieux. The *Confessions*, the story of Augustine's spiritual struggles, have secured a permanent place in great literature, spiritual or otherwise. The extent of St Augustine's influence, whether it be regarded as in all respects beneficial, is beyond argument.

Dr Grabowski, in his massive work, *The Theology of St Augustine*, is not exaggerating when he writes: 'There is something universal, even exceptional, about Augustine's place in the history of human thought.' He continues: 'In the course of the history of Christian thought in the West, Augustine's name has never been consigned to oblivion, never pushed to the background. To this day its lustre remains untarnished.'

Professor Daniel-Rops writes: 'Over a period of more than thirty years, Augustine appeared to his contemporaries as the conscience of the West, the beacon of the Church . . . the influence of St Augustine endured from century to century, increasing continuously. . . . This man who died so long ago still seems conspicuously present among us.' Fifty years ago when I was struggling for Christian belief Father Martin D'Arcy, SJ, placed the *Confessions* in my hands. It carried me into a different world and helped me enormously. Today I am too much worried by some of his views to appreciate him as once I did. But never for a moment would I doubt his claims to sanctity.

But what kind of saint was he and what made his religious influence so remarkable and so enduring? He cannot be encapsulated in a sentence. It can at least be accepted that his enormous intellect and literary genius were matched and inspired by an unsurpassed spiritual passion.

St Augustine was born at Tagaste in Numidia in AD 354. He died, aged seventy-six, in AD 430, having been Bishop of Hippo for the last thirty-four years of his life. His father, Patricius, who does not seem to have been a very agreeable character, became a Christian late in life. His mother, the future St Monica, comes down to us as a wonderful woman and most devout of Christians. At the age of twelve, Augustine went to a school of Grammar where he became steeped in Latin literature. He was never happy in Greek. At the age of seventeen he passed to Carthage. Formally made a Catachumen in childhood, he was not a Christian in spite of his mother's Christian influence. Following the custom of those around him, he took a concubine; before he was twenty he was the father of a boy, to whom he gave the name of Adiodatus.

Shortly afterwards he came under the influence of the Manichaeans. Peter Brown in his classical biography of Augustine describes the Manichaeans in this way: 'They were the "Bolsheviks" of the fourth century; a "fifth column" of foreign origin bent on infiltrating the Christian Church, the bearers of a uniquely radical solution to the religious problems of their age.' The Manichaeans were dualists, they believed that evil could not come from a good God. It came from an invasion of the good by a hostile force of evil, equal in power, eternal, totally separate, 'the kingdom of darkness'.

For nine years Augustine was a 'healer', looking forward to the possibility of joining the elect, but gradually he came to reject the whole system with contempt. He fell back then for a time on scepticism. 'Plagued by ambition and self-revulsion', to quote Daniel-Rops, he decided in AD 383 to go to Rome, but met with no success there. A year later he accepted an invitation to lecture at Milan. He was soon joined by his mother, now a widow. Her influence at this juncture was no doubt crucial. She persuaded him that he ought to marry. There followed the most unattractive action of his life. He packed off back to Africa his mistress, the mother of his child, the brilliant boy remaining with him. Nor did his frailty end there. While waiting to marry his young bride, he acquired another mistress. No one can deny that when St Augustine later preached on sin, he knew what he was talking about.

Still more obvious at this juncture was the influence of the statesman Bishop of Milan, Ambrose, later St Ambrose. During the period between then and his conversion, a matter of two years, Augustine soaked himself in Platonism, more particularly the neo-Platonic treaties, such as those of Plotinus. But Plato satisfied him no more than the Manichees. He quickly discovered the limits of Platonic metaphysics.

'It was impossible to "possess" the God of the Idealists. But was there not another God, who was the Word, and yet at the same time a living Presence, an answer to his love? And there, close at hand, was the mystery of the Incarnation. So Augustine turned at last to the Scriptures, those Scriptures that Ambrose expounded so lucidly. He read St Paul and found there the meaning of wisdom, not the wisdom described by the philosophers, but that expressed in the apparent folly of the Cross. "Thou hast concealed these truths from the clever and the wise, and hast revealed them to children." When Augustine read words like these, his soul trembled with anticipation; he was now very near to crossing the barrier which separated intellect from faith.'

But St Augustine could not cross the Rubicon and become a Christian by intellectual processes alone. He still faced grievous temptations, particularly of a sexual kind. He seemed incapable of overcoming his long-standing habits and emancipating himself from sin. 'I felt,' as he wrote in the *Confessions*, 'that I was still the captive of my sins and in my misery I kept crying: "How long shall I go on sinning? Why not make an end of my ugly sins at this moment?"'

One day he was with his beloved pupil Alypius in a garden, but had moved away from him so that he could cry to his heart's content. Tears were best shed in solitude. What happened next must be told in his own words: 'I was asking myself these questions, weeping all the while with the most bitter sorrow in my heart, when all at once I heard the singing voice of a child in a nearby house. Whether it was the voice of a boy or girl I cannot say, but again and again it repeated the refrain: "Take it and read, take it and read." At this I looked up, thinking hard whether there was any kind of game in which children used to chant words like these, but I could not remember ever hearing them before. I stemmed my flood of tears and stood up, telling myself that this could only be a divine command to open my book of Scripture and read the first passage on which my eyes should fall.'

He hurried back to the place where Alypius was sitting, where he had left the book containing Paul's Epistles. He seized it, opened it in silence and read the first passage on which his eyes fell: ' "Not in revelling and drunkenness, not in lust and wantonness, not in quarrels and rivalries. Rather arm yourselves with the Lord Jesus Christ; spend no more thought on Nature and Nature's appetites." I had no wish to read more and no need to do so. For in an instant, as I came to the end of the sentence, it was as though the light of confidence flooded into my heart and all the darkness of doubt was dispelled.'

Soon afterwards he took a reading party to Cassiciacum. From there he wrote to Ambrose asking to be received as a convert. At Easter AD 387 the Bishop himself baptised him along with Alypius and Adiodatus. He now resigned his Chair of Rhetoric and set out to return to Africa with Monica and some intimate friends. The projected marriage was forgotten. On the way Monica died waiting at Ostia for embarkation. Augustine settled with his friends on the small family estate at Tagaste, where they lived a common life of study and devotion. Within a year occurred the tragic death of Adiodatus at the age of seventeen.

St Augustine's reputation grew steadily. He was consecrated a bishop in AD 395 and became Bishop of Hippo a year later. In the next thirty-four years his influence spread far beyond his own diocese or even Africa. His letters, which have frequently been compared with those of St Paul, but which were far more numerous, went everywhere. He wrote book after book. The *Confessions* were written from AD 397 to 398; the twenty-two books, *The City of God*, were begun three years after the sack of Rome which took place in AD 410. They were issued separately as they were written, and finished in AD 426. It has been said that Augustine was seldom a systematic thinker. Whether or not that is altogether true, he was entangled in three great controversies. As priest and bishop, he found himself at grips with the Donatists. He had already, before leaving Rome for Africa, undertaken as a personal task the refutation of Manichaeism. The publication of his *Confessions* brought upon him a challenge from Pelagius, which lasted throughout the rest of his life. The first two issues are not of high concern today. The Pelagian issue will never, I would suppose, be disposed of.

Donatism had arisen at the beginning of the fourth century, following the Diocletian persecution. It was suggested that certain bishops were traitors. Having capitulated through the imperial agents, they were judged unworthy to direct the faithful and to administer the sacraments. Originating in an excessive scrupulousness, the Donatists had rapidly turned to schism, heresy and vicious attacks on the Catholics. The Manichaeans had attracted Augustine originally as explaining the most serious of all problems – that of evil. The Manichaeans declared the existence of two antagonistic entities and the opposition of matter to spirit. At one time they had seemed to Augustine to solve the enigma posed by Christianity with its purely spiritual God, but he had long since, by the time he became a bishop, totally rejected their position.

Dealing with the Donatists and the Manichaeans and, it must be added, the Pelagians, St Augustine showed a vehemence which today would be contrary to our ideas of Christian charity, but in those days seemed the clear course of duty. Pelagius was a British monk who will always be associated with an extreme emphasis on the freedom of the human will. He opened his attack at Rome, scandalised by the words: *Da quod iubes et iube quod vis* – Give what you order and order what you wish. Pelagius took this to involve a denial of freedom and responsibility. The crucial question then and now is how far a total acceptance of the will of God is compatible with human freedom.

Peter Brown, in his *Augustine of Hippo*, seems to me to sum up better than anyone else the issues at stake. Pelagius had claimed that the powers of human nature, originally created good by God, had admittedly been constricted by the weight of past habits and by the corruption of society. The remission of sins in baptism could mean for the Christian the immediate recovery of a full freedom of action. But Augustine's audience would be told repeatedly that even the baptised Christian must remain an invalid. Man's nature had been dramatically impaired by an event in the distant past. His recovery went far beyond his conscious choice. The cure for sin had to be far more radical than that proposed by Pelagius. The Christian life, as seen by Augustine, could only be a long process of healing. It is not surprising that Augustine has been frequently accused of pessimism – pessimism admittedly of man without God: but on a certain interpretation of St Augustine he shows a vast optimism about mankind redeemed by Jesus Christ.

I say 'on a certain interpretation' because Augustine's doctrine of predestination has given rise to never-ending controversies. 'It is,' writes Dr Grabowski, 'a most difficult if not impossible task to establish the meaning of St Augustine's concept of predestination in a manner which would satisfy all investigating minds.' Within the Roman Catholic Church, Augustinianism, Molinism and Thomism, differing in their explanations of the efficaciousness of grace, and in describing the nature of predestination, all invoke the authority of St Augustine in favour of their doctrine.

If I had to accept the plausible conclusion that St Augustine believed that God brought into the world large numbers of people whom he knew for certain would be damned for all eternity, I would be forced to have many reservations about the nobility of his outlook.

The City of God, all twenty-two parts of it, sets a difficult problem for those concerned primarily today with the sanctity of St Augustine. There can be no questioning its immense significance in the history of Christianity and Western culture. It represents a tremendous, indeed an heroic reply (taking thirteen years to complete) to the sack of Rome in AD 410. To quote Daniel-Rops: 'For a man of Augustine's stamp, the terrible event was much more than an occasion for lamentation. For a Christian, even the most frightful catastrophe had a meaning within the unfathomable intentions of God.' Man's proper task was not to mourn, but to build for tomorrow. The ultimate truth of God's purpose in St Augustine's eyes was assured.

The book is especially renowned for its famous delineation of 'the two cities' – the terrestrial city and the celestial city. They are fundamentally opposed to one another, since they are dependent on two quite contrary spirits. In practice, Church and State can collaborate; but we must never forget that the objects of their efforts are radically different. The Church is an organisation charged with the task of assuring the salvation of the faithful. She possesses special rights which cannot be challenged. It follows that the Church has special supervisory powers over the State. There is no doubt that the Church in the centuries that followed was permeated with this Augustinian doctrine.

To most of us, all this will seem to have little relevance today. We must remember, however, that the State in St Augustine's thinking was never identical with the terrestrial city. It was, to put it crudely, more virtuous. The Church was never equated with the celestial city. It was always less virtuous. We can still draw inspiration from the distinction between the two abstractions: the terrestrial city and the celestial city. For those of us who have been concerned with so-called practical politics in the second half of the twentieth century, St Augustine hardly provides a key to the more difficult problems.

Indeed, St Augustine's theology is today a matter of continuing controversy. An article in *The Tablet* by Professor Mahoney (10 May 1986) described him as 'a flawed giant'. But the last word may rest with Professor Henry Chadwick. After pointing out that no Western theologian writing about God had been able to escape Augustine's power, he concluded: 'That power came partly from his philosophical mind, deeply impregnated with the Platonic tradition, partly from his sheer mastery of words, but supremely from his own personal dedication. There was nothing half-hearted about his will to find perfect freedom in God's service.'

We are all familiar today with a recognition that Roman Catholic theology and, more widely, Christian theology, is not static but in a continuous process of development. We can admire therefore St Augustine's theology and his immense services to Christianity during his lifetime without accepting his views as binding on us at the present time. Some of them, as hinted earlier, especially when they relate to predestination, I find repulsive. But St Augustine the mystic, the spiritual writer, will appeal to us and strengthen us to the end.

It is time to turn to St Augustine the man. No bishop was, as far as we can judge, more loved by his flock, but many bishops have been loved by their flocks without being canonised. Daniel-Rops gives a moving picture of Augustine as he neared his end. The whole of Rome's African provinces was now at the mercy of the Vandals. The siege of Hippo had begun. The final outcome was all too obvious. In this beleaguered city, where defeatism had appeared so complete, there was one old man who was himself the incarnation of hope and courage. His final message expressed a strength of purpose which stemmed directly from God. These are difficult and dreadful times, it was said, but these times are part of us, are they not? The times are what we have made them. Yes, we are all guilty, but we have been promised mercy. Have you not been baptised in hope? Do you not understand that God's will can be accomplished through the most frightful afflictions?

Then the dying man begged God to forgive his sins. He reproached himself for not having done enough for him. This done, he ordered the penitential psalms to be nailed to the walls of his cell. Over and over again he repeated the verses fervently. On 28 August he died.

If we are to evaluate this man of God, we can prescind for a moment from his historic influence and even from his fairly controversial theology. Many of St Augustine's pregnant sayings have passed into the language:

> Thou hast made us for Thyself, and our heart is restless until it finds rest in Thee.
> This is the sum of religion, to imitate whom Thou dost worship.
> A man shall say unto me, *Intelligam ut credam* [Let me understand in order that I may believe]; and I will reply to him, *Immo crede ut intelligas* [Only believe that you may understand].
> There is one commonwealth of all Christian men.
> That heavenly city which has Truth for its King, Love for its Law and Eternity for its measure.
> Whosoever reads these words, let him go with me, when he is equally certain; let him seek with me, when he is equally in doubt; let him return to me when he knows his own error; let him call me back when he knows mine.

No single passage from his voluminous writings established more indisputably than the following his claims to be one of the greatest, if not *the* greatest of the mystics:

> Too late loved I Thee, O Thou Beauty of ancient days, yet ever new! Too late I loved Thee! And behold, Thou wert within, and I abroad, and there I searched for Thee; deformed I, plunging amid those fair forms which Thou hast made. Thou wert with me, but I was not with Thee. Things held me far from Thee, which, unless they were in Thee, were not at all. Thou calledst, and shoutedst, and burstedst my deafness. Thou flashedst, shonedst and scatteredst my blindness. Thou breathedst odours and I drew in breath and pant for Thee. I tasted, and hunger and thirst. Thou touchedst me and I burned for Thy peace.

Dom Cuthbert Butler, OSB, the author of *Western Mysticism*, calls him the 'Prince of Mystics'. He found in Augustine a 'unique form of combination of penetrating intellectual vision of spiritual things and passionate love of God'. Another commentator, Allison Peers, writing of St John of the Cross, places St Augustine on a pedestal along with St John and suggests that at certain points St Augustine went still deeper. One the other hand, Dean Inge, former Dean of St Paul's Cathedral, argues that it is hardly possible to claim St Augustine as a mystic at all.

The following is taken from St Augustine's account of his talk with his mother Monica just before her death:

> We, raising up ourselves, did by degrees pass through all things bodily, even the very heaven, whence sun and moon and stars shine upon the earth; yes, we were soaring higher yet, by inward musing, and discourse, and admiring of Thy works; and we came to our own minds, and went beyond plenty, where Thou feededst Israel for ever with the food of truth, and where life is the Wisdom by whom all these things are made, but is, as she hath been, and so shall she be ever.

There is yet one more reason why so many of us love St Augustine. His is not only the story of a sinner who became a great saint, but of a sinner who recognised that even after his conversion to Christianity the old temptations continued, losing little if anything of their potency. One of the most touching passages occurs in the tenth book, written long after his conversion, and referring to his subsequent temptations. 'Have pity of me, lord, in my misery. My sorrows are evil and they are at strife with joys of the good *and I cannot tell which will gain the victory*' [my italics]. St Augustine performs the miracle of soaring above us in his closeness to God and yet remaining in our midst as he struggles with the temptations which, in one form or another, are our constant affliction. Of all the saints, it is easiest to identify ourselves with St Augustine, along with St Peter.

5
ST PATRICK
c390(?)–461(?)

It would be inconceivable for anyone calling himself an Irishman, as I do, to omit St Patrick from his selection of saints. However, his inclusion here is not simply one of personal choice or nationalist sentiment. Patrick's position is secure as the effective founder of the Christian Church in Ireland and the patron saint of all thirty-two counties. Yet the difficulty of writing about him with any confidence is enormous, far greater than in other cases. The many learned scholars who have studied his life are divided on some of the crucial points. Indeed, hardly any aspect of his career is beyond dispute. It does seem that the *Confession*, a short memoir, and the *Letter*, a still shorter work, can be attributed to him, and I am also prepared to believe the same of the hymn in ancient Irish known as the *Lorica*, or *Breastplate*. To those may be added, if one so desires, the *Dicta Patricii*, five sayings preserved in the *Book of Armagh*.

St Patrick was probably born somewhere about AD 390 and died about AD 460. *Every Man's Book of Saints*, a companion volume to the Anglican *Alternative Service Book Calendar*, says of him: 'St Patrick was probably of Romano-British extraction, his father being both a Deacon and a municipal official.' Later on in the same book we read: 'Patrick, the Apostle of the Irish, was probably a Scotsman, though both England and Wales have always claimed to be his birth-place.' Professor Boin MacNeill, a great Irish scholar and a leading figure in the national resurgence, offers a different opinion. 'The most likely locality, in view of all the circumstances, would be somewhere near the shores of the Severn estuary.'

When Patrick was sixteen he was carried off by raiders and became a slave in pagan Ireland. For six years he herded swine or sheep, probably in Antrim, possibly also on the coast of Mayo. He turned to God, or maybe God turned to him. To quote the

Confession: 'Love of God and his fear increased more and more, and my faith grew and my spirit was stirred up, so that in a single day I said as many as a hundred prayers, and at night nearly as many, so that I used to stay in prayer even in the woods and on the mountains. And before the dawn I used to be aroused to prayer, in snow and frost and rain; nor was there any tepidity in me as now I feel, because then the spirit was fervent within me.'

The story of his rescue from captivity is vividly told in the *Confession*: 'One night I heard in my sleep a voice saying to me, "Thou fastest to good purpose, thou who art soon to go to thy fatherland." And again, after a short time, I heard the answer [of God] saying to me: "Lo, thy ship is ready." And it was not near at hand, but was distant, perhaps two hundred miles. And I had never been there, nor did I know anyone there. And thereupon I shortly took to flight, and left the man with whom I had been for six years, and I came in the strength of God who prospered my way for good, and I met with nothing to alarm me until I reached that ship.'

There he met with unexpected difficulties. The shipmaster told him, roughly and angrily: 'On no account seek to go with us.' But after Patrick had prayed they said to him, 'Come, for we receive thee in good faith, make friends with us in any way thou desirest.' Henceforth they set sail. 'And after three days we reached land and journeyed for twenty-eight days through a desert; and food failed them and hunger overcame them.'

The shipmaster at this point became extremely unpleasant. Patrick told him: 'Turn in good faith and with all your heart to the Lord my God, to whom nothing is impossible, that this day He may send you food in your journey until ye be satisfied, for He has abundance everywhere.' And by the help of God, Patrick tells us, it came to pass: 'Lo, a herd of swine appeared in the way before our eyes, and they killed many of them; and in that place they remained two nights; and they were well refreshed, and their dogs were sated, for many of them had fainted and were left half dead by the way. And after this they remained hearty thanks to God, and I became honourable in their eyes; and from that day on they had food in abundance. Moreover, they found wild honey, and gave me a piece of it. And one of them said: "This is offered in sacrifice." Thanks be to God, I tasted none of it.'

Where did Patrick land? On this point disagreement is wide-

spread. *The Alternative Prayer Book* says: 'They seemed to have
landed on the coast of Gaul. . . . Eventually Patrick was restored
to his family. . . . But there is evidence that St Patrick spent many
years in France.' Dr Hanson, in a learned treatise, is certain that
Patrick returned to Britain and is at least doubtful whether he ever
visited Gaul.

Patrick himself leaves the whole issue obscure until the moment
when he is recalled to Ireland in a night vision. 'After a few years I
was in Britain with my kindred, who received me as a son, and in
good faith besought me that at all events now, after the great
tribulations which I had undergone, I would not depart from them
anywhither. And there verily *I saw in the night visions* a man whose
name was Victorious coming as it were from Ireland with
countless letters. And he gave me one of them, and I read the
beginning of the letter which was entitled "The Voice of the
Irish", and while I was reading aloud the beginning of the letter, I
thought that at that very moment I heard the voice of them who
lived beside the Wood of Foclut which is nigh unto the western sea.
And thus they cried, as with one mouth: "We beseech thee, holy
youth, to come and walk among us once more."'

The circumstances attending his return are wrapped in obscurity. *The Alternative Prayer Book* says Patrick was over sixty when
he returned to Ireland, but this seems quite unacceptable. Hanson
places the return between AD 425 and 435, which would make
him thirty-five to forty-five. Luckily this need not affect our
appreciation of St Patrick, whatever chronology appeals to us. I
still find the narrative offered by Professor MacNeill half a century
ago the most attractive. We are confronted with the disconcerting
account provided in St Patrick's *Confession*. Something to his
discredit was discovered by the Elders who had to decide whether
or not to send him to Ireland. 'After the lapse of thirty years, they
found as an occasion against me a matter which I had confessed
before I was a Deacon.' It seems to be assumed that this was some
kind of sexual weakness. Be that as it may, there is no doubt that
Patrick was rejected.

The story of his humiliation and ultimate reinstatement is
conveyed in one of the most moving passages in the *Confession*. 'So
I was at first uneducated, an exile, ignorant indeed, one who
knows not to provide for the future, but this I know most certainly
that before I was humiliated I was like the stone that lies in the

deep mud, and He came, who is mighty, and in His mercy took me up and indeed verily raised me on high and set me on top of the wall.'

The following dates are speculative, but seem to point to the right sequence. In AD 430 the proposal to place Patrick in charge of the mission to Ireland was rejected. In AD 431 a certain Paladius was ordained Bishop by Pope Celestine and sent as first bishop to the 'Irish believing in Christ'. He reached Ireland in the year of his consecration, but by this time St Patrick, in his own words, 'was approved in the eyes of God and man'. On the journey to Ireland Patrick and those who were with him were met by clerics coming from Ireland who brought with them the tidings of the death of their Bishop, Paladius. In this new situation Patrick was consecrated Bishop and arrived in Ireland in AD 432. He was to remain there until his death thirty years later.

Patrick's own account of his Irish mission is brief: 'I came to the heathen Irish to preach the gospel and to endure insults from unbelievers, so as to hear the reproach of my going abroad [he refers here to his former slavery or perhaps simply to the taunt of being a foreigner] and to suffer many persecutions even unto bonds.' He tells of maidens converted who took vows of virginity, adding, 'not with the consent of their fathers, but they endure persecution and lying reproaches from their parents. Nevertheless their number increases more and more and we know not the number of our race [he refers here possibly to Britons in Ireland] who are there born again, in addition to widows and chaste living persons.'

An ultra-cautious scholar like Dr Hanson concludes: 'It is impossible to reconstruct Patrick's movements in Ireland.' Even Hanson accepts that Patrick 'probably did make his headquarters at Armagh'. There seems little doubt that this was so. He appears from the *Confession* to have educated the sons of local chieftains and others for the priesthood. Professor MacNeill points out that the choice of Armagh indicates that by AD 443, when Armagh was founded, Patrick's mission, starting in eastern Ulster, had already spread westward to a large part of the province.

For many years, however, it seems that the missionary work was chiefly successful in the eastern part of Ireland. The western half of the island is likely to have remained for a long time in the condition of a missionary territory. Two generations after Patrick's death, of

the twenty bishops two only are in Connaught and one in
Munster, whilst two others are in the middle part of Ireland. The
remaining fifteen belong to the eastern half. Patrick died, as
already mentioned, round about AD 460. It was said of him that
he resembled Moses in this among other respects, but 'where he
was buried, no man knows'. There is a strong tradition that it was
at Saul where his first church was founded.

Two other documents must be referred to in connection with St
Patrick's work, the *Letter*, which he eventually wrote himself, and
the *Hymn of Secondinus*, which has been accepted as contemporary
by some authorities if not by others. The event which called forth
St Patrick's *Letter* is quite well established. The soldiers of a British
tyrannus named Coroticus made a raid by sea on the Irish coast,
plundered the people of the district, who were Christians, some of
them recently baptised, slaughtered some of them and carried
away many others in captivity, taking with them also a large
booty. The captives were sold as slaves to the Scots and Picts, that
is to say, to the Irish colonists in south-western Scotland, and the
Picts in northern Scotland, these two peoples being at the time still
heathen. In the *Letter* Patrick demands the release of the captives,
and to compel their release and to deal properly with the crime he
demands also the excommunication of Coroticus and his followers.

One passage from Patrick's own account of the event gives us
some of its flavour. 'With my own hand I have written and
composed these words to be given and delivered and sent to the
soldiers of Coroticus – I do not say my fellow-citizens or the
fellow-citizens of the faithful Roman Christians, but those who are
fellow-citizens of the demons of their evil work. Behaving like
enemies, they are dead while they live, allies of the Scots and
apostate Picts, as though wishing to gorge themselves with the
blood of innocent Christians whom I, in countless numbers, have
begotten for God and confirmed in Christ.' There is no doubt that,
in keeping with the spirit of this *Letter*, Patrick played a large part
in securing the abolition of slavery in Ireland as a social
institution. In the seventh century, when the laws of Ireland began
to be written, they make no mention of legal slavery.

The *Hymn of Secondinus* arouses the usual controversy. Dr
Hanson, for example, refuses to accept it as a contemporary
document. He says: 'The authenticity of Secondinus's Hymn as a

document contemporary with Patrick has been accepted by several scholars – Todd, Bury, MacNeill, O'Rahilly, Newport White, Meissner, Grosjean and Bieler. But several weighty reasons make this very unlikely.' However, it seems impossible to ignore it altogether. Secondinus, one of the four bishops in the early years of Parick's mission, died in AD 447, eight years after his arrival in Ireland. MacNeill writes: 'There is no reason to question his authorship of the poem *In Praise of Patrick* which, in ancient tradition, describes him and him alone.'

Patrick in the poem is the apostle of Ireland, the founder of their Church. 'Constant in the fear of God and firm in faith, upon whom, as upon Peter, a Church is built, who has received from God his apostleship, against which the gates of hell do not prevail. The Lord has chosen him to teach barbarian heathens. . . . He has glory with Christ and honour in the world and is venerated by all as an angel of God. God has sent him like Paul, an apostle to the Gentiles.' The last lines of the poem led to the tradition that as the apostles on the Day of Judgment were to judge the twelve tribes of Israel, so Patrick on that day was to be the judge of the Irish nation: 'When he shall receive the reward of his immense labour, he shall reign with the apostles as a saint over Israel.'

What can one say of Patrick's abiding message? His best-known words are no doubt those of *The Breastplate*:

Christ with me, Christ before me,
Christ behind me, Christ in me,
Christ under me, Christ over me,
Christ to right of me, Christ to left of me.

Christ in lying down, Christ in sitting, Christ in rising up.
Christ in the heart of every person who may think of me!
Christ in the mouth of every one who may speak of me!
Christ in every eye which may look on me!
Christ in every ear, which may hear me!

Patrick had no pretensions to be any kind of academic theologian. The nearest he comes to a general theological statement is in paragraph 4 of the *Confession*, which must be given in full, as a summary of his credo:

Because there is no other God, nor was there ever any in times past, nor shall there be hereafter, except God the Father unbegotten, without beginning, from whom all things take their beginning, holding all things [i.e. Almighty] as we say, and His Son, Jesus Christ, whom we affirm verily to have always existed with the Father before the creation of the world, with the Father after the manner of a spiritual existence, begotten ineffably before the beginning of anything. And by Him were made things visible and invisible.

He goes on to say that Jesus Christ was made man and having overcome death was received into heaven by the Father. 'The Father gave to him power over things in heaven and things in earth and things under the earth'. Patrick moves to an exultant conclusion:

And let every tongue confess to him that Jesus Christ is Lord and God in whom we believe. And we look for his coming soon to be; the judge of the quick and the dead, who will render to every man according to his death. And He shed on us abundantly the Holy Ghost, the gift and earnest of immortality, who makes those who believe and obey to become children of God the Father and joint heirs with Christ whom we confess and adore as one God in the Trinity of the Holy Name.

Patrick was supremely a man of prayer. He saw visions and heard voices. His prayer was nourished on biblical imagery and biblical language. He was forever bemoaning his lack of education. There was no doubt, however, that he was steeped in his Latin bible, which he used in season and out of season for purposes of quotation. He is conscious at all times of God's mercies to him and, vastly more important, to the whole human race.

Dr Hanson suggests one interesting explanation of Patrick's undying appeal. He argues that, when Patrick was swept off into slavery at the age of sixteen, he suffered 'what we would now call a severe psychological trauma from which, in a sense, he never recovered'. As a result, Patrick, even as a venerable bishop, could never quite lose this image of himself as utterly helpless, utterly defenceless and abandoned. 'That is why we feel an inextinguishable sympathy with Patrick.' The inextinguishable sympathy will certainly always be felt whether or not we subscribe to the psychological explanation previously mentioned.

Patrick's humility, so patently sincere, makes an overwhelming impact from the beginning of his *Confession* to the end. The first words of the first chapter are: 'I, Patrick, the sinner and the most illiterate and the least of all the faithful, and contemptible in the eyes of fellow-men. . .'. Other saints and spiritual teachers have often spoken to the same effect without carrying the same conviction. Again and again, quite unselfconsciously he brings out his own profound sense of inadequacy, always returning to the strength given him by God, for which he deserves no personal merit. The last chapter of the *Confession* runs: 'But I pray those who believe in and fear God, whosoever shall have vouchsafed to look upon and receive this writing which Patrick the sinner, unlearned verily, composed in Ireland, that no one ever say it was my ignorance that did whatever trifling matter I did, or proved, in accordance with God's good pleasure; but judge ye, and let it be most truly believed that it was the gift of God. And this is my confession before I die.'

If Patrick were aware today of the innumerable men and women whose hearts have been won by his humility, he would not be displeased. He would attribute that quality of his entirely to God.

6

ST FRANCIS OF ASSISI
1181–1226

St Francis is, by common consent, the best-loved of all saints. He founded a world-wide order of a highly distinctive spirituality. He was canonized within two years of his death, more rapidly than happened before or has happened since. When in 1940 I was received into the Catholic Church by the Franciscan Capucins they happily ordained that my baptismal name, Francis, should become my name in the Church.

We can all discover our own St Francis. He was a mystic with a sublime gaiety and love of all human beings and animals, and indeed of the whole universe. He was a poet. He inspired large numbers of men and women to give away all that they possessed. He has been treated (by Lord Clark, in his book *Civilization*) as epitomizing the world of chivalry, courtesy and romance. It is as true today as when it was first said in the thirteenth century: 'No one can utter the name of St Francis without experiencing a certain sweetness.'

The best-known of all the incidents which illustrate his love of animals is the story of his preaching to the birds. By the wayside at Bevagna, some four hours' walk from Assisi, birds were gathered round some harvest sowing. Francis loved all nature, but birds to a special degree. They responded by coming to him without a trace of fear. 'My brother birds,' he said, when he saw them, 'you ought always to praise and love your Creator who has given you feathers for clothing, wings for flight, and all that you have need of. He has given you a dwelling in the purity of the air, though you sow not, neither do you reap.'

Another story of his friendship with creatures is almost equally famous. The town of Gubbio was much troubled by a fierce wolf that had already killed several men and made serious inroads on flocks. Francis, we are told, 'felt great compassion for the people of the place and, all alone, made his way to the wolf's lair'. He soon returned, the wolf trotting behind him. He persuaded the townsfolk to feed it. For two years until it died the wolf remained in Gubbio, an object of general esteem in the city. The artist Sassetta later depicted Francis with the paw of the wolf in his hand, while a notary draws up a treaty with it.

St Francis's love did not end with human beings and the animal creation. Everyone has heard of his *Canticle of the Sun*. Not so well known is the fact that when he wrote it in 1223 he was already virtually blind and in a state of advanced physical deterioration and extreme suffering. The *Canticle*, written in early Umbrian dialect, has often been described as the first great poem in the Italian language. No one admired it more than Dante.

Most High, all-powerful, all good, Lord!
All praise is yours, all glory, all honour
And all blessing.
To you alone, Most High, do they belong.
No mortal lips are worthy
To pronounce your name.
All praise be yours, my Lord, through all that You have made
And first my Lord Brother Sun.
Who brings the day; and light You give to us through him
How beautiful is he, how radiant in all his splendour.
Of you, Most High, he bears the likeness . . .

The hymn continues in praise of Brothers Wind and Air, Brother Fire, Sister Earth and, ultimately, Sister Death.

Of all the utterances attributed to St Francis the most eloquent is the incomparable *Prayer for Peace*. There is, to say the least, dispute as to whether St Francis wrote or dictated the actual words. No-one can doubt that it reflects his spirit. I have heard it used on a number of occasions with magical effect by the Ulster Peace People in their great rallies. When Mrs Thatcher became Prime Minister she enunciated it in Downing Street. A small book of mine on St Francis had been recently published, of which I sent her a copy. 'St Francis,' she replied, 'has always been one of my favourite saints.' There can be plenty of argument about the manner in which she has applied his teaching, none about the genuineness of her feeling for him. I cannot resist quoting the poem in full:

Lord make me an instrument of your peace.
Where there is hatred, let me sow love;
Where there is injury, pardon;
Where there is discord, union;
Where there is doubt, faith;
Where there is despair, hope;
Where there is darkness, light;
Where there is sadness, joy;
For your mercy and truth's sake.

O Divine Master, grant that I may not so much seek
To be consoled as to console,
To be understood as to understand,
To be loved as to love,
For it is in giving that we receive,
It is in pardoning that we are pardoned,
It is in dying that we are born to eternal life.

St Francis was born at Assisi in 1181 or 1182. His father was a
cloth merchant of Assisi, who carried on an extremely prosperous
business with the wealthier citizens. He imported his wares from
France and travelled there frequently, being in that country in fact
when Francis was born in Assisi. Francis's mother's name was
Giovanna; she is often referred to as Pica. It seems difficult to be
sure of anything else about her. It has been said that she was of
noble birth and of French origin, but there seems to be no evidence
for either statement. She is also described as quiet and pious,
which there is no reason to doubt.

'Francis,' to quote Butler's *Lives of the Saints*, 'was in his youth
devoted to the ideals of romantic chivalry propagated by the
Troubadours. He had plenty of money and spent it lavishly, even
ostentatiously. He was uninterested alike in his father's business
and in formal learning.' When he was about twenty, war broke out
between the cities of Perugia and Assisi. Francis, who had fought
with the cavalry, was taken prisoner by the Perugians.

For a year he was held in captivity. On his release he was struck
down by a long and dangerous illness. Somewhere between the
end of 1203, when he returned from captivity, and 1206 he
underwent a profound conversion. This did not occur in a single
flash, but rather a series of 'divine strokes' or visitations. Still
intent on becoming a knight, St Francis was ready to join a
military expedition which would link up with an army fighting on

the Pope's behalf in the south of Italy. Now came the first of the divine strokes.

One night, shortly before starting out, he had a vision of his Lord. While Francis was asleep a man appeared who called him by his name and led him into a vast and pleasant palace. The halls were hung with glittering coats of mail, shining bucklers and all the weapons and armour of the warriors. Francis asked excitedly what the meaning was of all this. For whom were the arms and the palace intended? He received the answer that they were for him and his knights. When he awoke in the morning he took this literally to mean that he was going to achieve great success in the war, and so set off for Apulia via Spoleto, as originally intended.

On his arrival at Spoleto Francis felt unwell. He thought with apprehension about the journey ahead and retired to bed. Then, half asleep, he heard a voice calling, asking him where he was heading. He replied, describing his plans. The voice continued: 'Who do you think can best reward you, the master or the servant?'

'The master,' answered Francis.

'Then why do you leave the master for the servant, the rich lord for the poor man?'

'O Lord, what do you wish me to do?'

'Return to your own place and you will be told what to do. You must interpret your vision in a different sense. The arms and the palace are intended for other knights than those you had in mind; and your principality too will be of another order.'

Francis at once obeyed the instruction. He abandoned the expedition and returned home. He was well received by his friends, but he was not quite the Francis they had known. He was still at certain moments the prince of fun-makers, at other times he seemed far away.

Then came the second and still more dramatic stroke. On an evening of jollifications, Francis had been elected master of the revels. The young men of Assisi were parading after a feast through the streets of the city with Francis bringing up the rear, carrying his wand of office. Suddenly, in the words of the chronicler, he was 'visited of the Lord'. He was rendered totally immobile. He said afterwards that 'had I been pricked as with knives all over at once, I could not have moved from the spot'. His companions missed him and came back to look for him. They found him in a trance-like state. 'Are you in love, Francis?' they teased him. 'Yes,' he said, 'I am in love with a bride nobler, richer and fairer than you have ever seen.' The bright young fellows laughed heartily; but Francis kept his thoughts to himself.

Francis quickly ceased to visit his former friends. He sought out the poor, frequently giving them his clothes, to his own discomfort. He made the pilgrimage to Rome and to the tomb of St Peter. When he saw the crowds of beggars gathered in front of the church he was moved, 'partly', we are told, 'by the attraction he felt in his devotion and partly by the love of poverty' to give his clothes to one of the poorest around him. Then he dressed in the beggar's rags and spent the whole day among the crowd there, filled with an 'unaccustomed joy of spirit'.

Soon he faced the hardest test of his whole life. One day, as he was riding on the plain before Assisi, he met a leper. To quote from the testament he wrote just before his death: 'When I was yet in my sins, it seemed to be unbearably bitter to look at lepers. And then the Lord led me into their country and I showed mercy to them. When I went away from them, that which had at first seemed bitter to me was now changed for me into sweetness of soul and body.' The actual event was traumatically brief. Francis dismounted from his horse; he walked up to the leper then slowly and deliberately kissed his hand. A day or two later he visited the leper house and went round to each of the sufferers, kissing each man's hand and placing a coin in it.

By this time, on the ethical plane, he had crossed the Rubicon. It needed, however, a third stroke to demonstrate what God demanded, and even that was not to be conclusive. Francis left the town one day to meditate out of doors. As he was passing the church of St Damian which was threatening to collapse with age, he felt the urge to go in and pray. As he knelt in prayer before the image of Christ crucified, he heard a voice coming from the Cross telling him three times: 'Francis, go and repair my house, for you see that it is all falling down.' He rose to his feet in an ecstasy of joy. Here was the answer to his repeated prayers: the divine task pointed out to him beyond any possibility of mistake. He seems to have had no doubt at the time that the church was St Damian's. It may be that a wider vision occurred to him later.

He seems to have had no hesitation about collecting bales of cloth from his father's warehouse, selling them for a large sum of money and pressing it on the priest at St Damian's. To his credit, the priest refused it. Francis's subsequent dispute with his father culminated in a painful and not very edifying scene. The bishop told Francis to hand back anything which belonged to his father. Stripping off his clothes, Francis laid them with the money at the bishop's feet. 'My lord,' he said, 'I will gladly give back to him not only the money that belongs to him but my clothes also.' Then, turning to address the crowd that had gathered: 'All of you, listen and understand. Up till now I have called Pietro Bernardone my father; but since now I intend to serve the Lord I give back to him the money about which he was so angry, and all the clothes which I have had from him. I wish to say only: "Our Father which art in Heaven", not "my father, Pietro Bernardone."' With this symbolic gesture, Francis won the sympathy of the crowd. His father departed, a discredited figure; but Francis embarked on a lifetime of self-renunciation.

In a spiritual sense, Francis was committed to his life's vocation. After finding sanctuary in the leper house he returned to Assisi, assumed a hermit's habit and began to repair the church of St Damian. He no longer had any money at his disposal, nor any goods which he could sell. If the church were to be rebuilt it had to be done by his own hands 'for the love of Christ poor and crucified'. He overcame his embarrassment and took to begging from those who had known him as a wealthy young man, in order to obtain the necessary materials.

St Francis duly completed the rebuilding of San Damiano. Then he made his way to a little chapel called Portiuncula, which stands in a plain two miles from Assisi and was at that time in ruins. He repaired it and went to live close by. Here, on the Feast of St Matthias in the year 1209, his way of life was shown to St Francis. In those days, the gospel of the Mass on this feast was Matthew x, 7–19: 'And going, preach saying: The Kingdom of Heaven is at hand . . . . Freely have you received, freely give . . . . Do not possess gold . . . . nor two coats, nor shoes nor a staff. . . . Behold I send you as sheep in the midst of wolves. . .' . The words went straight to his heart and, applying them literally to himself, he gave away his shoes, staff and girdle, and left himself with one poor coat which he girt about him with a cord. This was the dress which he laid down for his friars the following year, the undyed woollen dress of the shepherds and peasants in those parts.

A number of admirers soon wanted to be companions and disciples of St Francis. The first of these was Bernard da Quintavalle, a rich tradesman of Assisi. Bernard sold all his effects and divided the sum among the poor. Peter of Cattaneo, a canon of the cathedral of Assisi, also wanted to be with him, and Francis 'gave his habit' to them both together on 16 April 1209. The third to join them was Brother Giles, a man of great simplicity and spiritual wisdom. When his followers had increased to a dozen, Francis drew up a short informal rule consisting chiefly of the gospel counsels of perfection. In 1210 he took this to Rome for the Pope's approbation. Innocent III afterwards told his nephew, from whom St Bonaventure heard it, that in a dream he saw a palm tree growing up at his feet, and in another he saw St Francis propping up the Lateran Church, which seemed ready to fall. He therefore sent for St Francis and approved his rule, but only by word of mouth, tonsuring him and his companions and giving them a general commission to preach repentance.

Now that the Pope's sanction had been obtained the movement expanded with astonishing rapidity. The friars were soon to be seen on the roads not only of Italy but of all Europe. In the years ahead they would make their way to North Africa and, somewhat later, to India and China. Within fifty years of the saint's death there were over fifty communities in England and more than five hundred in Italy.

The first few years of the period following have been described as the idyllic time of the Order. Numbers were growing and already the great names of Franciscan history were gathered round the Founder. But numbers were not yet a problem. The inevitable dilemma of how to run a world-wide Order while retaining the principles worked out for a handful of saints raised its head gradually.

No essay on St Francis, however brief, would be complete without some reference to St Clare. This remarkable woman, a fellow citizen of St Francis, became his disciple and was, in a sense, co-foundress of his Order. She lived for nearly thirty years after Francis's death, fighting for the things Francis had held so dear, fighting even the popes themselves to establish his ideals but remaining throughout a loyal daughter of the Church. 'As long as I live,' she declared, 'St Damian's will remain a fortified tower of supreme poverty.' Francis had willed it and to him she would be loyal unto death. 'He for God only, she for God in him.' In the words of Francis's earliest biographer, Thomas Celano: 'She was one of those great souls the human tongue cannot worthily praise.'

The first general chapter was held at Portiuncula at Pentecost in 1217 and in 1219 a chapter was held called 'of mats', because of the number of huts of wattles and matting hastily put up to shelter the brethren: there were said to be five thousand of them present. In June 1219, following this chapter, St Francis set sail with twelve friars and came to Damietta on the Nile delta before which the crusaders were sitting in siege. Francis made his way to the presence of the Sultan, but was equally disappointed in him and in the crusaders.

Summoned by an urgent message of distress, he returned to Italy. He found that in his absence his two vicars had introduced innovations whose tendency, according to Butler's *Lives of the Saints*, was to bring the Franciscans into line with other religious orders and to confine their proper spirit within the more rigid framework of monastic observance and prescribed asceticism. Francis set to work to revise the rule. Finally, in 1223, it was approved by Pope Honorarius III. It has been argued that the original spirit of Franciscan revolution had been lost; certairly Francis was not happy with it.

The Christmas of 1223 he spent at Greccio in the valley of Rieti. A 'crib' was set up at the Hermitage; the peasants crowded to the midnight Mass, at which Francis served as deacon and preached on the Christian mystery.

Towards the Feast of the Assumption in 1224, he retired to Mount Albernia and there made a little cell, alone except for Brother Leo. On or about Holy Cross day 1224, the miracle of the stigmata occurred. While he was engaged in prayer on the mountainside, Francis saw a seraph with six fiery wings coming down from the highest point in the heavens. Then he saw the image of a man crucified in the midst of the wings, with his hands and feet stretched out and nailed to a cross. Francis was filled with wonder. While still in a state of bewilderment, the marks of the nails began to appear on his hands and feet, just as he had seen them a little while before in the crucified man above him. His right side was as though it had been pierced with a lance. The wound frequently bled, so that his clothing was often covered with blood. Francis, thus marked with the sign of the Passion of Jesus Christ, tried to conceal what had happened – 'this favour of Heaven', in Butler's words – and ever after covered his hands with his habit and wore shoes and stockings on his feet.

The two years that remained of his life mingled suffering and happiness in God. His sight was failing, but he was not to be deterred from his labours. He travelled widely through Umbria. He was brought to St Damian's where the future St Clare nursed him for six weeks. It was there, in this sad physical condition, that he wrote the immortal *Canticle of the Sun*.

It seemed that the end could not be far off. He was still grieving over what he considered his defeat in the argument over the rule. The doctor told him that he could not live much longer. His response was immediate. Yet another verse flowed from his lips:

> Praised be You, O my Lord, for Sister Bodily Death
> Whom no man living can escape,
> Woe to those who die in mortal sin,
> But blessed those who find themselves according to Your Will
> For them no second death shall harm.

Angelo and Leo sang it for him. In Francis joy and sorrow were always close together but never so close as at that moment.

At last he was allowed to return to his beloved Portiuncula. As he was carried down to the woods he turned and gave his final blessing to Assisi. Death was near; but in the last few weeks, perhaps in the last two or three days of his life, he still found energy and inspiration to produce his unforgettable *Testament*. It has been represented as in conflict with the rule which he had accepted, not without reluctance, in 1223; but this is unconvincing. The *Testament* is not intended to be a systematic summary, however brief, of Francis's teaching. This passage alone should make that clear:

> The friars should not say this is another Rule. For this is a reminder, admonition, exhortation, and my Testament which I, Brother Francis, worthless as I am, leave to you, my brothers, that we may observe in a more Catholic way the Rule we have promised to God. The minister-general and all the other ministers and custodes are bound in virtue of obedience not to add anything to these words or subtract from them.

Francis sent a last message to St Clare and her nuns:

I, little Brother Francis, wish to follow the life and poverty of our most high Lord Jesus Christ and of His most holy Mother, and to persevere in it until the end. And I beg of you, my ladies, and I give you counsel, that you live always in this most holy life and poverty, and take much care of yourselves lest, by the doctrine or advice of anyone, you ever depart from it.

On Thursday 1 October he requested the brothers to strip him and lay him on the ground so that he could die in real poverty. Then he blessed them, one by one. Next day he broke bread with them, stretched out his arms over his brethren in the form of a cross and blessed all the friars both present and absent. Then he said: 'I bid you goodbye, all you my sons, in the fear of God. Remain in Him always. There will be trials and temptations in the future, and it is well for them who persevere in the life they have undertaken. I am on my way to God, and I commend you all to his favour.'

He called for a copy of the Gospels and asked to have read the passage from St John which begins: 'Before the Pascal feast began.' (John xii, 1). With his failing strength, he intoned the psalm: 'Loud is my cry to the Lord, the prayer I utter for the Lord's mercy' until the last verse: 'Too long have honest hearts waited to see you grant me redress' (Psalm 141). He passed away peacefully on 3 October 1226, dying as he had lived in absolute humility and poverty; naked, on the naked earth.

This short outline of his life should leave no doubt as to why St Francis has occupied a unique position in the affections of succeeding generations. St Bonaventure, writing the major life of St Francis within forty years of his death, singles out certain qualities in particular for chapter headings: 'The Austerity of his Life'; 'His Humility and Obedience'; 'His Love for Poverty'; 'His Loving Compassion'; 'His Devotion to Prayer'; but the message has proved much more controversial than the man. During his lifetime he was made unhappy by the thought that the purity of his doctrine of poverty was being diluted. After his death the controversies multiplied. The Franciscan Order remains one of the chief missionary orders in the Catholic Church. It has missions in Africa, India, the Far East and the whole of Latin America. The dedication to social reform and the relief of distress have never wavered; but the division between the Observants, the Conventuals and the Capuchins would have distressed St Francis.

In any treatment of the doctrine of St Francis poverty takes its place in the forefront, but as soon as that word is mentioned the controversies begin.

In a deep sense, Francis embraced poverty not only in the interests of the poor but as an essential part of his own spiritual life. He believed, without finding it necessary to argue the point, that Christ himself was the prototype of a poor man. He was also convinced that riches stand between their possessor and God; in other words, that they are a major spiritual menace. Here the Gospels can be readily quoted: 'Blessed are the poor . . .'; 'It is easier for a camel to go through the eye of a needle than for a rich man to enter the Kingdom of God'; and so on. Disciples of St Francis can argue to the end of time whether one should be prepared to give up riches if they happen to come one's way, or whether one should refrain from seeking them. One can at least be certain that in all such matters he would have been stricter than St Francis de Sales or other famous Christian writers.

Francis drew sublime inspiration, as mentioned above, from what Christ said to the young man in the Gospel: 'You need only one thing: go and sell all you have and give the money to the poor and you will have riches in Heaven. Then come and follow me.' He himself carried out that instruction to the letter in his own life. It is perhaps astonishing that a world that has seldom tried to practise it should yet continue to offer unique homage to the author of the message. The life of St Francis is some explanation, but one is bound to seek for something deeper. His combination of joy and self-denial takes us part of the way, but it is impossible to appreciate St Francis to the full without linking his whole life and teaching to those of Christ. Without the Passion, the life of Christ would be diminished out of recognition. We do not begin to appreciate the real significance of St Francis if we do not realise that he shared to the full, again as far as any human being can, not only the beauty but the agony of Christ's mortal existence. Without that agony, Christ could not have redeemed us; without his share in it, St Francis could not have played his part down the centuries as the unique messenger of divine love.

7
ST CATHERINE OF SIENA
1347–1380

St Catherine of Siena was born in 1347 and died thirty-three years later. She is, by common consent, one of the greatest of the saints. One cannot help comparing her with Joan of Arc. Joan made a tremendous impact on the political and military situation of her time. She too died young, at nineteen. She was not looked upon as a saint during her lifetime, though she began to be referred to as such after she had been burnt. She has left us an heroic, rather than a spiritual memory. Catherine of Siena, in contrast, was widely recognised as a saint during her lifetime and has left us a spiritual message which is as alive as ever.

St Catherine figures prominently in the secular history of the fourteenth century. She is well described by Barbara Tuchman in her arresting book about that century: 'Since June 1376, Catherine of Siena, who was to be canonised within a century of her death, and ultimately named patron saint of Italy along with Francis of Assisi, had been in Avignon exhorting the Pope to signal reform of the Church by returning to the Holy See.' Already, at the age of twenty-nine, she possessed an ardent following. She was revered for her trances and raptures, and her claim to have received, whilst in ecstasy after Communion, the stigmata of the five wounds of Christ on hands, feet and heart.

Catherine's larger mission in her own mind, again quoting Barbara Tuchman, was 'an apostleship for all humanity through her own total incorporation with God and Jesus and through a cleansing and renewing of the Church.' Her authority was the voice of God speaking directly to her, and preserved in the *Dialogues* dictated to her secretary-disciples. They were believed by Catherine to have been 'given in person by God the Father, speaking to the mind of the most glorious and holy virgin, Catherine of Siena . . . she being entranced the while and actually hearing what God spoke in her.'

Two days after her arrival in Avignon Catherine was presented by Fr Delle Vigne, her spiritual director, to Pope Gregory XI. She had, to quote from Alice Curtayne's classical biography, 'written to him six times in an intolerably dictatorial fashion. "I have heard that you have created cardinals. I believe that it would be more to the honour of God and better for yourself if you would always take care to choose virtuous men. When the contrary is done, it is a great insult to God and disaster to Holy Church. We must not be surprised afterwards if God sends us his chastisements and scourges, for it is but just. I beseech you, do what you have to do manfully and with the fear of God."'

The tone of this communication (by no means the sharpest) is certainly amazing. This woman of twenty-nine could never have sent it unless she had had clear proof already in their brief correspondence that her words carried tremendous weight with the head of the Roman Catholic Church. We must step back to trace some of the steps by which Catherine had achieved this extraordinary position.

Catherine was born Catherine Benincasa. Her father was a wool dyer. She was the twenty-fourth of twenty-five children, but her father was able to maintain his large family in middle-class comfort. He owned the large house in which he lived and the workshops in which he ruled over a number of apprentices. He also had a farm and vineyard. Catherine was thus born into the class that ruled the city. A brother of hers became at one time one of the twelve governors of the commune. There was little in her background, however, which, on the face of it, equipped her to give advice to a pope or to the crowded heads of Europe.

There is a story of a vision she had when aged seven, but there was nothing unusual about her until, at the age of sixteen, she took the traumatic step of becoming a solitary. She trained herself in asceticism until she could live on a spoonful of herbs a day and a couple of hours' sleep at night. For three years she lived in entire seclusion in her own room. She never went out except to go to the nearby Dominican church; she spoke to no one except her confessor. There was an understandable opposition from her family, but she clung to her self-imposed solitary existence until she was nineteen. Then, to general amazement, she returned to family life, took her share in the work of the home and began to do voluntary nursing in the city hospitals.

What caused such a decisive change? On Shrove Tuesday
1366 she prayed for unassailable faith, asking fervently to be
delivered from her recurrent doubts. Then, to quote again from
Alice Curtayne:

> Into that cold, dark chamber advanced with solemn majesty a pageant
> incomparably more gorgeous than anything seen on the streets of
> Siena. Preceded by dazzling light, celestial music, with warmth,
> perfume, colour and sheer joy (all that she was so heroically denying
> her senses) there came towards her the Redeemer, His Blessed
> Mother, St John, St Paul, St Dominic, David and legions of angels.
> While the grave and kindly looks of this heavenly cohort were bent
> upon her, with the formality of a betrothal ceremony, she received the
> eternal assurance of Christ that, as she was espoused to Him in faith,
> his strong support would never fail her.

From this ecstatic vision she recognised clear intimation from
God that her life of seclusion was to end. Without hesitation she
walked into the kitchen – to the astonishment of her family, who
were busy eating their dinner.

Within a few months she had achieved a remarkable position in
Siena. She became heavily involved in ecclesiastical and com-
munal affairs – all the more remarkable since she had grown up
unable to read or write. Even so, she acquired a fluent knowledge
of Latin. A growing circle of followers now gathered round her.
They were a varied band of men and women, anxious to serve her
devotedly in return for what she would teach them about the
Christian way of life. Her young men were called 'Caterinati', but
she called them, simply, her family. Their own humorous epithet
for themselves was the '*bella brigata*'. Ecclesiastical history has
rewarded this strange club with the noble title 'School of Mystics'.

The fame of Catherine's visions and fastings spread far and
wide. Between her raptures she was accepted as a model of
common sense, a person to whom people readily brought their
quarrels. From 1370 on she took an increasing part in public life,
exhorting rulers, prelates, town councils and individuals in
eloquent letters of political and spiritual advice. 'Do God's will
and mine,' she commanded Charles V in one letter urging a
crusade. To the Pope in the same tone she wrote: 'I demand that
you set forth to fight the infidel.'

But she did not neglect the poor, the sick or prisoners close at hand. She was the occasion of many spectacular conversions. One of the best-known is that of Niccolo di Toldo. Di Toldo was a young Perugian aristocrat who, at a public banquet in Siena, had made a contemptuous reference to the Sienese government. For this he was arrested and condemned to death – brutal treatment even by the standards of those days, particularly given the strained relations between Siena and Perugia.

Catherine was appealed to and went at once to the prison. She told the whole story in one of the best-known of her letters:

> I went to visit him of whom you know; whereby he was so comforted and consoled that he confessed and prepared himself right well. And he made me promise for the love of God that, when the time of execution came, I would be with him. And so I promised and did. . . . I waited for him, therefore, at the place of execution. Then he came like a meek lamb and, seeing me, he laughed. He asked me to make the sign of the cross for him. I did so and said: 'Up to the nuptials, sweet brother, for you are soon to be in everlasting life.' He knelt down with great meekness and I stretched out his neck and bent down over him, reminding him of the Blood of the Lamb. His lips said: 'Jesus, Catherine.' So saying, I received his head into my hands, closing my eyes in the Divine Goodness and saying: 'I will.' . . . Then I saw God-and-Man, as one sees the splendour of the sun, receiving that soul in the fire of his divine charity.

After his execution her soul afterwards reposed in peace and quiet in such fragrance of 'blood' (incidentally one of her favourite words) that she could not bear to have removed from her garments the blood that had fallen on them. And then this extraordinary characteristic revelation: 'Wretched and miserable, I remained on earth with the greatest envy.'

The intricacies of Italian politics were intertwined with Catherine's public career at every point. The Italian states were bitterly resentful of the control exercised by the papal legates, the latter being French at a time when the papacy was located in France. Most of the cardinals belonged to that nation. The so-called Tuscan League was indeed at war with the papacy. The prevailing anarchy in Italy could be attributed, not unreasonably, to the exile of the papacy in Avignon.

In the spring of 1376 the feud between the city and the papacy worsened. The Signori of Florence sought the aid of Catherine's influence in winning release from the interdict under which they had been placed. Catherine consented to go to Avignon to plead the cause of Florence. When she arrived she found that the Florentines had already disowned her. Nothing daunted, she turned her attention to wider concerns – above all, the return of the papacy to Rome. The Pope was, in any case, well-disposed to the idea of return, but Catherine made a great impression on him, and strengthened his purpose. 'Mysterious and very fruitful' was her summary of her stay in Avignon. She was an object of vulgar curiosity on the part of many of the women of Avignon who gathered in church to see her, and were rewarded by the sight of her passing into an ecstasy while she received Communion. One woman went so far as to stick a knife into her foot.

The Pope made his triumphant entry into Rome on 16 January 1377. The city, however, was divided into bitter factions; the health of the Pope steadily declined and he did not live for long.

The conclave that followed his death was chaotic. The Roman populace insisted that they must have an Italian pope. Eventually a Neapolitan, Urban VI, was elected, but the French cardinals, who were in the majority, soon expressed regret that they had elected him, and announced that the Holy See was vacant. Urban's immediate reply was to nominate twenty-three new cardinals. The Frenchmen then went into conclave and elected a rival pope. The great Western schism which was to last for seventy years emerged in its full horror.

Catherine was naturally overwhelmed with grief. A saying soon began to go round: 'Better a pope in exile than two popes.' She was widely blamed for persuading Gregory XI to return to Rome, thus promoting the split. She was convinced that she had served the Church well, but that was not how the matter was seen at the time. She wrote to Urban VI offering her life and the lives of her friends in the cause of truth, and was soon summoned to Rome. The new pope had great confidence in Catherine's powers because of her international standing; he received her willingly and in the ensuing months saw her frequently.

Catherine wore herself out on behalf of the Roman papacy. She sent out letters all over Christendom, imploring help for the head of the Church. Nevertheless the position deteriorated. Every diocese was soon divided on the issue, every parish, every religious community. Catherine's own family failed signally to rise to the occasion. On the fifth Sunday of Lent 1380, while praying in St Peter's, she suffered a stroke and had to be carried home. She died three weeks later, aged thirty-three, and was canonised eighty-one years after her death.

While waiting to be called to Rome for the last time, she dictated to three secretaries her book *The Dialogue*, which sets out to give the world some account of her mystical creed. She finished it in four days, during which she herself took no rest. It has always been accepted as one of the great works of mysticism, and continues to be translated and re-edited in all the languages of the modern world.

It has been asked before now how she managed to find space for the mystical in a life so short yet so feverishly filled with activity. It seems to be agreed by all, however, that had it not been for her mystical experience she would never have been capable of her immense activity. Her spiritual adviser, Raymond of Capua, has written: 'Being so closely associated with her I was able to see at first hand how, as soon as she was freed from the occupations in which she was engaged for the work of souls, at once, one might almost say by a natural process, her mind was raised to the things of heaven.' It was precisely what she experienced in contemplation that impelled her into action. Her contemplation was so present in her active life that she prayed and even burst into ecstasy within the text of many of her letters.

There has been considerable argument about Catherine's central motive. Some critics have said that it was the desire for truth, others contend it was love. As has been well said by Suzanne Noffke, OP, in her notable introduction to her translation of Catherine's *Dialogue*, both motives are central to her. The way to God for Catherine is the constantly lived dynamic of knowledge and love:

> A soul rises up, restless with tremendous desire for God's honor and the salvation of souls. She has for some time exercised herself in virtue and has become accustomed to dwelling in the cell of self-knowledge, in order to know better God's goodness towards her, since upon knowledge follows love. And loving, she seeks to pursue truth and clothe herself in it.

Another matter discussed among students of Catherine concerns the origin of her powerful teaching. She had no formal schooling, yet her teaching can be described as at once Thomist and non-Thomist. Suzanne Noffke recognises multiple influences: Augustine, Cassian, Gregory the Great, Bernard, Francis, Thomas, Ubertino, Passavanti, Cavalca, Colombini. For someone who learned to read so late there is something almost miraculous here. Incidentally scholars at that time taught and wrote in Latin, yet all she wrote and dictated was in her own Sienese dialect. *The Dialogue* is her crowning work.

Suzanne Noffke rejects the common belief that Catherine dictated *The Dialogue* entirely in the space of a single five-day ecstasy. She considers that a much longer time was involved, probably close on a year. There is no doubt, however, that in the end much of it was dictated whilst she was in ecstasy. Her disciple Caffarini writes:

> I say also that I have very often seen the virgin in Siena, especially after her return from Avignon, rapt beyond her senses, except for speech, by which she dictated to various writers in succession, sometimes letters and sometimes the book, in different times and in different places, as circumstances allowed.

It is a hopeless task in an essay such as this to convey the overwhelming spirituality of *The Dialogue*. It begins with a prologue in which the fundamental argument of the whole book is encapsulated in the opening paragraphs. Here we have the interplay of truth and love already referred to, but also the beauty and dignity of the human creatures whose perfection is in union with God. She then enumerates the four petitions she addressed to God. The first is for herself (later there is a plea that she be allowed to suffer in atonement for her sins and those of humanity); the second is for the reform of the Church; the third is for the whole world and especially for peace in relation to rebellious Christians; and the last is for Divine Providence in all things.

The second chapter is called 'The Way of Perfection'. God replies briefly to her first petition. He instructs her on:

- the need for infinite desire in relation to finite works;
- the role of one's neighbours in the economy of charity;
- the virtues;
- discernment as the lamp and 'seasoning' of all the other virtues.

In the third chapter Catherine formulates three petitions. She asks for mercy for the people of God, for the mystic body of the Church, for mercy for the world and for grace to follow the truth. God responds by telling of the gift of the redemptive blood of Christ and the responsibility that that gift imposes. He speaks also of the way of truth, that is to say, the bridge of Christ.

The fourth chapter deals in detail with this bridge. It is often described as the central and most important part of the whole work. The fifth chapter describes the five kinds of tears. The sixth, entitled 'Truth', indicates the three lights by which we see – the imperfect, the perfect and the most perfect. The seventh chapter begins with a tremendous eulogy of the priesthood and the eucharistic mystery. God treats at length the sins of evil clerics. Divine Providence is the subject of the eighth chapter. The ninth deals with obedience. In the tenth, called 'Conclusion', God summarises the content of the whole book and Catherine responds with thanks and a hymn of praise to the Trinity. She closes with a prayer that she may be clothed in truth.

God says to Catherine: 'You asked four petitions. The first was for yourself. I have satisfied this by enlightening you with my truth and showing you how you might come to know this truth that you longed to know. I explained to you how to attain knowledge of the truth through knowledge of yourself and of me by the light of faith. The second thing you asked me was that I should be merciful to the world.' He continues: 'Your third petition was for the mystic body of the Holy Church. You begged me to relieve her of darkness and persecution and wanted me to punish you for the sins of others.' God says that on this matter He had explained to her that no suffering given in finite time could itself atone for sins committed against the infinite good, but such suffering could atone if it was united with the soul's desire and heartfelt contrition in a manner that He will explain. 'In my immeasurable mercy and love for human kind, I sent the Word, my only begotten Son. And to show it to you really clearly, I set him before you in the image of a bridge stretching from heaven to earth through the union of my divine nature with your human nature.'

God goes on to explain how the bridge is mounted by three stairs, the soul's three powers. At each stage he shows Catherine what it is that takes away the soul's imperfection and makes her attain perfection. In regard to the fourth petition, he explains his providence in general. He goes on to tell her about the perfection of obedience and the imperfection of disobedience. 'Now in conclusion,' he says, 'I, the eternal Father, supreme eternal truth, am telling you that in the obedience of the Word my only begotten Son, you have life.'

Truth, he goes on, is founded on the living rock. 'The gentle Christ Jesus, clothed in the light, can discern darkness. Clothe yourself in this light, dearest daughter, whom I so love in truth.'

Catherine replies with a glowing hymn of praise. 'You responded, Lord: you yourself have given and you yourself answered and satisfied me by flooding me with a gracious light, so that with that light I may return thanks to you. Clothe, clothe me with yourself, eternal Truth, so that I may run the course of this mortal life in true obedience and in the light of most holy faith.'

I knew little of St Catherine of Siena before I began work on this book. She emerges as my favourite saint. All the saints considered here leave an impression of having been close to God all or part of their lives. No saint was ever more certain that he or she had been conversing with God than St Catherine. No saint leaves an impression of having been more close to Him or perhaps even quite as close.

8

ST JOAN OF ARC
1412–1431

St Joan is unique among all the saints canonised by the Roman Catholic Church, in that she made an immediate and extraordinary impact upon the political and military situation in her time. She is generally accepted, even by humanists, as the national saint of France. Frenchmen are entitled to feel that she played a supreme part in liberating their country. Five centuries later, they still feel as the British felt about Winston Churchill immediately after the Second World War, though the parallel between the French burning Joan and the British ousting Churchill in the General Election of 1945 can hardly be pressed. Churchill had been a Cabinet Minister on and off for thirty years. Joan was a peasant girl of seventeen in her year of tremendous victories, 1429. She could initially neither read nor write, nor ride a horse, though she became a first-class horsewoman. She was soon leading the French army to triumph in battle, and standing beside the King of France when he was crowned in Rheims.

Such a figure could be conceived in myth or legend. That her life actually happened still seems barely credible. In her arresting book on Joan, Marina Warner heads her last chapter 'Saint or Patriot?' She leaves her readers to make up their own minds. She suggests, however, that no recognised label will satisfactorily apply. Joan's claim to be called a patriot and a great one is indisputable; her claims to sanctity must be considered controversial, but they have been judged sufficient.

Many English people have acquired their main appreciation of Joan from Bernard Shaw's memorable play. It is convenient for our present purpose to divide her life into five acts:

1 Born 6 January 1412. Childhood and youth till she leaves home aged seventeen in 1429.
2 February–July 1429. Great victories under Joan's leadership. Charles VII crowned King of France.

3 September 1429–May 1430. Joan unsuccessful in battle. Captured
   at Compiegne.
4 May 1430–May 1431. Joan on trial. Joan at the stake.
5 (a) 1455–1456. Verdict on Joan rescinded.
   (b) 1920. Joan canonised.

The main outline of her life-story is well known, though on one
point (her temporary recantation) there is considerable disagreement. Sainte Jeanne la Pucelle, or Joan of Arc as she has always
been called in England, was born on the Feast of Epiphany at
Domremy, a little village of Champagne on the bank of the Meuse.
She was one of five children. Her father was a stern peasant
farmer, her mother gentle and affectionate. At this time France
was torn by civil war between the contending parties of Burgundy
and Orleans. Burgundians threw in their lot with the English. The
defeat of the Burgundians and the eviction of the English were
therefore part of the same Orleans objective.

Joan was in her thirteenth year when she experienced the
earliest of her supernatural manifestations. 'God sent a voice to
guide me,' she said at the trial. 'At first, I was very much
frightened. The voice came towards the hour of noon, in summer,
in my father's garden. I had fasted the preceding day. I heard the
voice on my right hand, in the direction of the church. I seldom
hear it without [seeing] a light. That light always appears on the
side from which I hear the voice.'

Whatever the nature of the voices and however they arrived,
they had come to stay. As Vita Sackville-West puts it in her *Life of
Saint Joan*: 'Once they had begun, they never left her. She heard
them with increasing frequency and clarity. At first she was
frightened and doubtful, and could not understand what was
happening to her; then after she had seen her first strange visitant
several times, she decided that he was no other than St Michael.
Asked how she had finally decided on his identity, she replied that
she recognised him at last because he spoke with the tongue of
angels.' We know from Joan's evidence at the trial far more than
would otherwise have been possible. Three spirits habitually
appeared to her – the Archangel Michael, St Margaret and St
Catherine. She claimed also to have seen the Archangel Gabriel
and several hundreds of other angels, but it was with her three
familiars that she was chiefly concerned. She saw them with her
bodily eyes, and wept when they left her, wishing that they could

have carried her away with them. They came always accompanied by the cloud of heavenly light. She could touch them and embrace them.

Joan was positive that she had seen, heard, touched and even smelt them, not once or twice but daily, hundreds of times, in fact, over a period of seven years. Gradually they unfolded the charge laid on her. By 1428 they had become insistent and explicit. She must present herself at once to Robert Beaudricourt who commanded the King's forces in the neighbourhood. This she duly did. He was sceptical at first, saying that her father ought to give her a good hiding, but she refused to be put off indefinitely. Finally, Beaudricourt gave her an escort of three men-at-arms to take her to the French King.

She travelled in male dress, which she adhered to passionately thereafter. Marina Warner dwells learnedly on the significance of her male costume. In Butler's *Lives of the Saints* we are told simply that 'she travelled in male dress to protect herself.' After studying the various theories, I am inclined to agree with those who see it as her way of insulating herself from sexual harassment and dedicating herself exclusively to her divine mission.

On 6 March 1429 she was admitted to the royal presence. Charles had disguised himself, but she identified him at once and made an immediate impression on him by revealing something which he supposed was known only to himself. 'Sire,' she said, 'if I tell you things so secret that you and God alone are privy to them, will you believe that I am sent by God?' He seems to have encouraged her to proceed. She thereupon informed him of prayers that he had privately offered on the last All Saints Day. It did not take long after that for him to come to believe in the supernatural nature of her mission.

Then, with amazing audacity, she asked him for soldiers whom she might lead to the relief of Orleans. In spite of opposition from many of the courtiers, Charles gave his consent. Arrangements were pushed forward to equip her to lead an expeditionary force. A special standard was made for her, bearing the words 'Jesus: Maria', together with a representation of God to whom two kneeling angels were presenting a fleur-de-lis.

On 27 April the army left Blois with Joan at its head, clad in white armour, and on 29 April she entered Orleans. Her presence in the city wrought marvels. By 8 May the English forts which surrounded Orleans had been captured and the siege raised, although Joan herself was wounded in the breast by an arrow. Within days, however, she led a brilliantly successful campaign on the Loire, ending with a crushing victory over the English at Patay. On 17 July Charles was solemnly crowned at Rheims with Joan standing at his side with her standard. That event, which completed the mission originally entrusted to her by her voices, marks the close of her military successes. A boldly planned attack on Paris failed – mainly, it is argued, for lack of Charles's promised support. On this occasion Joan was wounded in the thigh and had to be dragged to safety by her friend the Duke of Alençon.

A frustrating winter of inaction followed. Upon the resumption of hostilities Joan hurried to the relief of Compiegne which was holding out against the Burgundians. She entered the city at sunrise on 23 May 1430, and that same day led an unsuccessful sortie. The drawbridge over which her company was retiring was raised too soon, leaving Joan and some of her men outside at the mercy of the enemy. She was dragged from her horse and led to the quarters of John of Luxembourg, one of whose soldiers had been her captor. From that time until the late autumn she remained the prisoner of the Duke of Burgundy. Never during that period or afterwards was the slightest effort made on her behalf by King Charles or any of his subjects.

On 21 November she was sold to the English, who were determined to have her sentenced as a sorceress and a heretic. She appeared for the first time during a tribunal presided over by Peter Cauchon, Bishop of Beauvais, who hoped, it is said, through English influence to become Archbishop of Rouen. The judges were composed of dignitaries and doctors carefully selected by Cauchon, as well as of the ordinary officials of an ecclesiastical court. During the course of six public and nine private sessions, the prisoner was examined and cross-examined about her visions and 'voices', her assumption of male attire, her faith and her willingness to submit to the Church. At the conclusion of the sittings a so-called 'summing-up' of her statements was drawn up and submitted to the judges. On the strength of it they declared her revelations to have been diabolical. She was then passed to the University of Paris, which denounced her in violent terms.

It is difficult to distinguish the political from the religious considerations at work in her trial. There was no doubt that the

English were determined that, one way or another, Joan should be destroyed, having first been discredited. The attitude of her ecclesiastical judges was more complicated. They certainly wished to discredit her, but they were also – though it is hard to believe this now – genuinely concerned to save her soul.

The conditions of her imprisonment were appalling. To quote Vita Sackville-West again: 'She had now known captivity for some seven months, but never captivity such as this. Spiritually and physically she suffered as she had never suffered before. Spiritually, she was now denied all the comforts of the Church. Physically, she was denied the privilege which should have been accorded her as one about to be tried by the Church, of being kept in the ecclesiastical prison, where the Bishop of Rouen had at his disposal a room for women, and where she might have been placed under the care of women; but was thrown, instead, in irons into a common cell.' There seems little doubt that she was chained to a block of wood. She may well have been denied a bed, except possibly when she fell ill.

In the final scene, the tribunal unanimously decided that if the prisoner persisted in her refusal to retract she must be considered a heretic, sorceress and apostate. In a word, she was determined in their view to set her own voices above the wisdom of the Church. When the final sermon was over, she was yet again asked to submit her words and deeds to the Church. She replied in keeping with the answers many times given during the trial: 'I will answer you. As for my submission to the Church, I have already given them my answer. Let all my words and deeds be sent to Rome, to our Holy Father the Pope, to whom, after God, I will refer myself. As to what I have said and done, I have done it through God. I charge no one, neither my King nor any other; if there is any fault, it is mine alone.'

The Bishop of Beauvais began to read the final sentence. 'For these reasons we declare you excommunicate and heretical, and pronounce that you shall be abandoned to secular justice, as a limb of Satan severed from the Church. . .' .

Suddenly Joan broke down. We must remember that she was a totally convinced and committed Catholic and that to die with the Catholic anathema resting on her was a spiritual torture of which a non-Catholic could hardly conceive. She gave way completely until, in Vita Sackville-West's words: 'Nothing was left of her

TOP:
The Crucifixion of St. Peter, by
Michelangelo

CENTRE:
St. Peter Repentant, by Goya

RIGHT:
St. Augustine of Hippo, by Botticelli

ABOVE LEFT:
St. Francis of Assisi (1181–1226)

ABOVE:
St. Catherine of Siena (1333–1380)

LEFT:
St. Joan of Arc (1412–1431)

ABOVE:
St. Thomas More (1471–1530) in prison, with his daughter, Margaret

RIGHT:
St. Ignatius Loyola (1491–1556)

St. Frances de Sales (1567–1622) as
depicted by Murillo

St. Theresa of Avila (1515–1582)

St. John of the Cross (1542–1591)

proud denials.' She would defer in all things to the Church and her judges. She would no longer support or believe in the apparitions and revelations she had pretended to have. She said this several times over, as though she wished to make quite sure that she had been perfectly understood, and said again in everything she would follow her judges and the Church.

She was led back to prison, but her respite was a short one. In circumstances that are by no means clear she resumed the male dress which she had consented to discard. When Bishop Cauchon visited her in her cell, he found that she had recovered from her weakness. She was asked: 'Since last Thursday, the day of your abjuration, have you heard the voices of the saints Catherine and Margaret?' 'Yes,' she replied. 'What did they say to you?' 'They told me that through them God sent me his pity of the betrayal to which I consented in making the abjuration and revocation to save my life and that in saving my life I was damning myself. . . . If I were to say that God had not sent me, I would be damning myself, for it is true that God did send me. My voices have told me since then that I did very wrong in doing that which I did and that I must confess that I did wrong. It was fear of the fire which made me say that which I did.'

On Tuesday 29 May 1431 the judges, after hearing the bishop's report, condemned her as a relapsed heretic and the following morning, at eight o'clock, having been handed over to the secular authorities, that is to say the English, she was burned at the stake in Rouen. The executioner was afterwards both frightened and contrite, saying he was damned, having burned a saint, and that God would never forgive him. He said that in spite of all the oil, sulphur and fuel he had used, he could not reduce her entrails or her heart to ashes. He had thrown everything which remained of her into the Seine.

She was only nineteen years old.

Twenty-three years later, Joan's mother and her two brothers appealed to Pope Callistus III for a re-opening of the case. Butler's *Lives of the Saints* reports briefly: 'On 7 July 1456 the labours of the commission resulted in the quashing of the trial and verdict and the complete rehabilitation of the Maid.' Marina Warner is at pains to stress the political, rather than the religious influences at work. 'Charles VI wanted the English who had rigged Joan's trial discredited and his good name thereby rehabilitated.' Be that as it may, the rehabilitation of Joan was on paper complete.

It took, however, another 464 years for canonisation to be achieved – in 1920. Beatification had been accorded eleven years earlier. By this time Joan had in terms of devotion become France's national saint, revered alike by patriots, liberals (who admired her stand against the tyranny of the Church), and feminists of all kinds, a saint like St Teresa of Lisieux and the great mass of Catholics who identified with her readily. The Vatican might be thought to have had a small problem because she had been burnt after being found a heretic by the Inquisition, even though this verdict had been set aside. But this problem was overcome without much difficulty.

It was decided that the Rouen judges of 1431 were adherents to the schismatic Council of Basle. The canonisation decree, however, rested heavily on the evidence of the rehabilitation and does not quote Joan in person at all. It mentions the extraordinary marvels of her skill in horsemanship, the supernatural signs at her death, her heart unconsumed in the ashes. Her loyalty to the Catholic Church itself is necessarily stressed. Her confessor was always 'at her side'. Marina Warner reminds us also that Joan is not a 'martyr of the Church'; she is not officially designated a witness to the faith at the hands of its enemies. In the Calendar she is simply a 'virgin'; but that after all she always saw as essential to her divine mission.

From the above it should be obvious that Joan was a heroine, but was she anything more? In the last resort, if we are going to call her a saint, where do we find the special justification? Vita Sackville-West writes: 'For me there is only one comprehensive, stupendous unity of which we apprehend but the smallest segment. My readings into Joan of Arc have done nothing but increase my belief in the existence of that unity, and also the belief that certain persons are in touch with, or, shall we say, receptive to the influence of, a unity for which we have not adequate name, the greater whole of which our own imagination embraces but a tiny part.'

There is certainly nothing incompatible here with the Christian view that Joan's unbelievable life-force sprang from a divine source, best called in this connection the Holy Spirit.

9
ST THOMAS MORE
1478–1535

The most popular saint in the world is probably St Francis of Assisi. But if serious-minded Englishmen were asked to choose their favourite *English* saint St Thomas More would surely be their choice. Indeed, a wider claim can be made for him. Dr Johnson said he was 'the person of greatest virtue these islands ever produced.' If the question took the form of: 'who is the greatest Englishman?' St Thomas More would stand a good chance against Shakespeare, Wellington and Winston Churchill. But one must distinguish between popularity and sanctity. The former derives from all that we know of his entire life. The latter did not emerge until near the end.

Something of his quality can be seen from one of the last of his public utterances. He had been tried and found guilty on perjured evidence and condemned to death. The penalty for treason was to be hanged, drawn and quartered. In fact, Henry VIII planned to permit him to be executed with an axe, the privilege of a peer, but More could not have known that at the time.

His final words to his judges were these:

> The blessed apostle St Paul, as we read in the Acts of the Apostles, was present, and consented to the death of St Stephen, and kept their clothes that stoned him to death and yet be they now both twain Holy Saints in Heaven, and shall continue there friends for ever, so I verily trust and shall therefore right heartily pray, that though your lordships have now here in earth been judges to my condemnation, we may yet hereafter in Heaven merrily all meet together to our everlasting salvation.

Here was a man with many brilliant talents. He wrote the Latin classic, *Utopia*, as widely read today as ever; but admirers of that book will hardly argue that it strengthens More's claim to sanctity. Of his other books some, in their attacks on heretics, make painful reading today; others, such as *The Dialogue of Comfort*, written in his prison cell, are profoundly inspiring.

The first fifty-one years of More's life culminated in his

appointment as Lord Chancellor, in 1529. Six years later he was beheaded. By the time he became Lord Chancellor, St Thomas was probably the most acute legal intellect of his time. He was hardly less eminent as a classical scholar. He was much loved by his family and a wide circle of friends, including the supreme humanist, Erasmus. His wit was proverbial and has travelled well down the centuries. Yet if he had died before his imprisonment and execution his chances of canonisation would have been extremely slight. It was his Christian bearing which has placed him on a pedestal of his own.

It is certainly remarkable on the face of it that More should occupy such an extraordinary position in the admiration of Englishmen. After all, he was executed because he refused to accept the Protestant revolution initiated by Henry VIII. And England from that day to this, with a short Marian interlude, has remained Protestant, or at least non-Roman Catholic. It is usually considered that he is a supreme example of a man who laid down his life in response to the dictates of conscience; and Englishmen are disposed to feel that his manner of doing so was very English. But even here there is room for controversy.

Dr Anthony Kenny, one of More's many biographers, agrees that on one interpretation More can be made to appear a forerunner of modern ideas of toleration and respect for sincerity, and the contemporary notion that each man must make his own moral decisions for himself. In these respects More's attitudes seem to contrast with the intolerance and authoritarianism of the mediaeval Church and the Renaissance state. But Kenny feels that this impression is misleading. For him, says Kenny, the human conscience was not an autonomous law-giver. A man's conscience was his belief, true or false, about the law made by God. To act against conscience was always wrong, because it was acting against what one believed to be God's law. But to act in accordance with his conscience was not necessarily right, for one's conscience might be an erroneous opinion. One had a duty to inform one's conscience correctly.

More was no undiluted admirer of popes. He was living in the worst period of the Vatican's history. Yet, in Kenny's words: 'It was the Papal supremacy for which he died.' Even in its worst times, the universal authority of the papacy had been a symbol of the essential unity of Christian people in a single Commonwealth

A map of Utopia, from the original edition

of Christendom. In the last analysis, therefore, More died for the unity of Christendom.

What do we learn from Thomas More's writings? His best-known work, *Utopia*, is a futuristic fantasy, and helps us little in our study of sanctity. Utopia itself is an imaginary island containing fifty-four cities, each surrounded by twenty miles or so of agricultural land. There is no private property and no money. Unlike Plato's *Republic*, in More's Utopia the primary social unit is the family or household. Unlike most of their neighbours, the Utopians are monogamous, and marriage is in principle life-long. However, adultery may break a marriage; the innocent, but not the adulterous, spouse is allowed to remarry. Besides adultery, 'the intolerable wayward manners of either party' provide grounds for divorce and the remarriage of the unoffending spouse. On rare occasions divorce by consent is permitted. The islanders thank God that they belong to the happiest commonwealth and profess the truest of all religions. But they know nothing of Christianity and we are left quite uncertain as to whether More is making theoretical proposals for a new kind of society or satirising those societies which already exist.

The other topic which must unavoidably be touched on is More's long series on heretics, some of which at least can only be called vitriolic. No one who sets out to write a full biography of More can skate over his record in this area at all lightly. Kenny sums up More's record as Lord Chancellor in this way: 'As a judge, he was active in enforcing the laws against heresy, especially when he later became Lord Chancellor. During his Chancellorship six heretics were executed. Not a large number, say some of his apologists, but then, in Wolsey's much longer Chancellorship, none were [sic] executed at all. More was personally involved in detecting three of those six cases. He would not have thanked those modern biographers who have sought to play down his zeal against heresy.'

Kenny less convincingly argues that More regarded heresy in the same way as a modern liberal magistrate regards racist propaganda, something disgusting and corrupting in itself, likely to lead to civil discord and violence and therefore needing to be firmly stamped out. Maybe so; but modern magistrates, liberal or other, would shrink back in terror from the methods adopted by More and his contemporaries. It would be agreeable to persuade ourselves that in the last few months of More's life he repudiated attitudes which are to us so unacceptable, but there is no evidence of this. We are left with the unattractive role of congratulating ourselves on the progress made between his century and ours. We can remind ourselves that even saints are in many ways limited by the attitude and prejudices of their time and culture.

Thomas More was born in Milk Street in the City on 7 February 1478. At fourteen, he was placed in the household of the future Cardinal Morton, Archbishop of Canterbury. This early contact with the greatest in the land was brought about through the influence of his father, Sir Thomas, then a rising barrister and afterwards a Justice of the Court of the King's Bench. He was sent, perhaps a year later, to study at Oxford; Canterbury College later absorbed in Christ Church, claims him. Dr Kenny indicates that possibly he attended Magdelen College School. More, however, stayed at Oxford less than two years. He must have 'gone down' when he was about sixteen. He was later derisive of the poor fare and equally poor logic taught there. Yet by the time he was twenty-five, though a lawyer by profession, he was 'one of the most accomplished classical scholars of his generation' (Kenny).

There was a moment when it seemed that More would give himself over to an ascetic life. He took a lodging near the Charterhouse and subjected himself to the discipline of a Carthusian monk. He wore a shirt of hair next to his skin. He scourged himself every Friday and on other fasting days, went to sleep on the ground with a log under his head and allowed himself only four or five hours' rest. This phase lasted about four years, 1499–1503. He then abandoned all idea of 'leaving the world', but to the end of his life he was scrupulous in the observance of his religious duties.

The year 1504, More's twenty-sixth, was an important one for him. He was a regular visitor at the house of John Colt, a wealthy landowner living in Essex who had three handsome daughters. More, according to his son-in-law, William Roper, was most attracted by the second as 'the fairest and best favoured'; yet when 'he considered that it would be both great grief and some shame also to the eldest to see her younger sister in marriage preferred before her, he then of a certain pity framed his fancy towards her.'

Jane, his final choice, bore him four children, of whom the eldest, Margaret Roper as she became, has passed into history.

Jane herself, according to Erasmus, was growing into an ideal intellectual companion to More when in 1511, still in her early twenties, she died. More remarried within the month. His bride was Alice Middleton, a prosperous merchant's widow who brought into the family a solid dowry. More himself is said to have called her ungallantly 'neither a pearl nor a girl'. Poor Dame Alice, as she came to be called, has had a bad press. On a charitable view, there was a genuine affection between her and her husband, but other views have been not uncommon.

With the coronation of Henry VIII in 1509 good prospects opened up for More in the law courts. In that year he was elected a Bencher of Lincoln's Inn, and in 1510 was appointed Under-Sheriff of London. The King and Wolsey soon took notice of him. A Privy Councillor in 1517, he was soon being used on various missions. He was knighted in 1521 and elected Speaker in 1523; in 1525 he was appointed Chancellor of the Duchy of Lancaster. The King began to come to More's house in Chelsea. William Roper mentions one of these visits when the King, after dinner, walked in the garden for about an hour, with his arm round More's neck. More's comment, when Roper congratulated him afterwards, was characteristic: 'I thank our Lord. I find his Grace my very good Lord indeed; and I believe he doth as singularly favour me as any subject within his realm. Howbeit, son Roper, I may tell thee I have no cause to be proud thereof, for if my head would win him a castle in France it should not fail to go.'

Soon the King became determined to rid himself of his wife Catherine of Aragon and to marry Anne Boleyn. He was determined to secure ecclesiastical sanction for divorcing Catherine. Wolsey, for so long the second man in the kingdom, made no progress with the Pope. Additionally, the Peace of Cambrai in 1527 was regarded by Henry as a humiliation. Henry stripped Wolsey of the office of Chancellor and charged him in 1529 under an old statute of accepting papal appointments. More was appointed in his place, the first layman to hold the Chancellorship.

More cannot be deemed to have worked for or even to have welcomed the post. He was already unhappy about Henry's proposed divorce of Catherine, and received an assurance from the King that he would not be expected to take any part against his conscience in proceedings about 'the great matter of divorce'.

Nevertheless, no admirer of More can fail to ask: 'was it really right for More to accept the Chancellorship in these circumstances?' In 1985 the American scholar, Richard Marius, published a comprehensive *Life of More*. Marius, whose admiration for More is limited, not surprisingly attributed More's acceptance of the office to personal ambition, in part at least: 'Here was a promotion he could hardly turn down, a remarkable and unforeseen culmination to all those years as an obedient royal servant, shifted here and there in the apparatus of government as his superiors found him useful. Given Wolsey's enormous power in the office, More must have supposed that his own authority would also be great, and he enjoyed authority, an important place in the world.'

Marius is fair enough to add that, apart from personal ambition, More must have seen the office as a commanding height from which to protect the Church from its many enemies, a divine commission to do what he could to save a bad situation, perhaps even a divine call. If we are going to judge More's attitude to heretics by present-day standards we should ask ourselves what a present-day public man would have done in his place. It would be very strange if such a one had declined the office of Lord Chancellor. Still, we are not discussing the average politician or statesman, we are talking of a man destined to become a glorious saint. One should of course bear in mind the sense of enormous loyalty to Henry, inexplicable to the present writer, which was expressed by More, even in his dying moments. What one cannot measure today is how far such a percipient man saw the noose into which he was putting his head.

The next six years can be divided into two halves: 1529–1532, with More as an active Lord Chancellor; and 1532–1535, with the steady pressures bringing him to the scaffold. As Lord Chancellor More carried forward certain reforms which Wolsey had introduced to bring justice within reach of the poor, but meanwhile laws causing him much distress were passing through Parliament. In 1529 the Commons passed a series of bills reducing the influence of the clergy. Wolsey died in 1530; a few weeks later the King accused the whole clergy, as he had formerly accused Wolsey, of violating the *Statute of Praemunire* by exercising jurisdiction in church courts. The clergy in the Canterbury Convocation sued for pardon, offering to pay a fine of £100,000; but this was not enough for Henry. They had also to accept him as the 'only Supreme Head of the English Church'. This was eventually accepted by the clergy, but with the qualification: 'as far as the law of Christ allows'. In May 1532 the King demanded that all future clerical legislation in Convocation should receive the royal assent. The bishops made a show of resistance, but on 15 May they once again caved in. Thomas More could take no more and resigned.

He explained to his family in his whimsical way that most of his income had disappeared. To quote Roper again: ' "I have been brought up", quoth he, "at Oxford, at an Inn of Chancery, at Lincoln's Inn, and also in the King's Court, and so forth from the lowest degree to the highest, and yet have I in yearly revenue at this present little above an hundred pounds by the year, so that now must we hereafter, if we like to live together, be contented to become contributaries together." ' The end, at least in retrospect, should have appeared inevitable with a man like Henry VIII in control.

The pressures mounted remorselessly. In June 1533 Henry's new wife, Anne Boleyn, was to be crowned in Westminster Abbey. More refused to be present. He told a story which implied that the bishops might be deflowered by countenancing the King's new marriage. 'And when they have deflowered you, then they will not fail soon after to devour you.'

It seemed increasingly certain that More himself would be devoured. He defeated attempts to have him convicted of taking bribes and of association with Elizabeth Barton, the so-called 'maid of Kent'. He wrote to Henry VIII reminding him that he had cleared himself and went on to say: 'Our Lord for his mercy send you I should once meet with your Grace again in Heaven, and there be merry with you, where among mine other pleasures this should yet be one, that your Grace should surely see then that (however you take me) I am your true headman now and ever have been, and will be till I die, howsoever your pleasure be to do by me.'

It was More's last letter to the King. He was to die with the King's name on his lips. I find it impossible even to begin to guess the real state of his feelings towards Henry. Those who were destroyed by the monarch of the day were expected, like Russians in the pre-war trials, to praise their destroyers. Did he really admire Henry at all?

The noose was soon tightened. The Parliament that met in January 1534 passed an Act to regulate the succession to the throne. It declared that the marriage between Henry and Catherine was against God's law, and was utterly void notwithstanding any licence or dispensation. It fixed the succession on the offspring of the marriage with Queen Ánne; on the eldest surviving son, if there should be one; or, if not, on the Princess Elizabeth. Catherine's daughter Mary was passed over.

More was summoned to appear at Lambeth Palace, to take the oath prescribed in the Act. This he refused to do, explaining his attitude to his daughter Margaret a few days later: 'I showed unto them that my purpose was not to put any fault either in the Act or any man that made it, or in the oath or any man that swore it, nor to condemn the conscience of any other man. But as for myself in good faith my conscience so moved me in the matter that, though I would not deny to swear to the succession, yet unto the oath that there was offered me I could not swear without the jeopardy of my soul to perpetual damnation.'

More was willing, we have noted, to swear to the succession, because it was within the competence of Parliament to determine that. But the validity or invalidity of a marriage was a religious matter: it would be defying God to endorse a falsehood.

The King, not surprisingly, insisted on the full oath. It was tendered to More again on 17 April. He again refused it, as did Fisher, and the two were immediately committed to the Tower. Roper recalls his wife's first visit to her father, after he had been a prisoner for about a month. 'I believe, Meg,' said Sir Thomas, 'that they that put me here, ween they have done me a high displeasure. But I assure thee, on my faith, my own good daughter, if it had not been for my wife and you that be my children, whom I account the chief part of my charge, I would not have failed long ere this to have closed myself in as strait a room and straiter too. I find no cause, I thank God, Meg, to reckon myself in worse case here than in my own house. For me thinketh God maketh me a wanton, and setteth me upon his lap and dangleth me.' That remained his spirit to the end.

Even Roper and Margaret did not fully appreciate the working of Thomas's conscience, still less did his wife, Dame Alice. When she visited him she marvelled, 'you who have always been hitherto taken for so wise a man will now so play the fool to lie here in this close filthy prison and be content thus to be shut up among mice and rats.' More replied, after some further discussion: 'For I see no great cause why I should much joy either of my gay house or of anything belonging thereunto, when, if I should but seven years lie buried under the ground, and then arise and come hither again, I should not fail to find some therein that would bid me get out of doors, and tell me it were none of mine. What cause have I then to like such an house as would so soon forget his master?'

In the seventh session of the Reformation Parliament which opened in November 1534, four Acts were passed which bore on More's fate: (1) the Act of Supremacy, which declared that the King was supreme head of the English Church and rejected all foreign authority in ecclesiastical matters; (2) a second Act of Succession which regularised the oath enacted under the previous Act; (3) a new Act of Treason which made it treasonable to deprive the King of any of his titles, including the title conferred by the Act of Supremacy; and (4) an Act of Attainder against More, Fisher and five other non-juring clergy.

More was interrogated by Thomas Cromwell and other members of the Council. However, they failed to trap him into any direct denial of the supremacy. He was asked why if he was, as he said, ready to die, he did not speak out plainly against the statute. 'I have not,' he replied, 'been a man of such holy living as I might be bold to suffer myself to death, lest God, for my presumption, might suffer me to fail.' In other words, suicide remained in his eyes a sin.

In July he was brought to Westminster Hall for a state trial. He still refused to give a direct answer to the question of whether he did or did not accept the supremacy of the King in religious matters. But now a lying witness was produced, the Solicitor-General Richard Rich. He had interviewed More in prison and attributed to him what was regarded as a damning admission: 'No more than Parliament could make a law that God were not God could Parliament make the King Supreme Head of the Church.' More vigorously denied that he had made any such statement, but the blatant perjury sealed his fate. When he was convicted he insisted in making a statement in which he at last revealed his true position: 'Forasmuch as this Indictment is grounded upon an Act of Parliament directly repugnant to the laws of God and His Holy Church, the supreme Government of which, or of any part whereof, may no temporal Prince presume by any law to take upon him, as rightfully belonging to the See of Rome, a spiritual pre-eminence by the mouth of our Saviour himself, personally present upon earth, only to Saint Peter and his successors, bishops of the same See, by special prerogative granted, it is therefore in law, amongst Christian men, insufficient to charge any Christian man.'

Facsimile of an engraving made in Antwerp in 1587, commemo-rating the beheadings of John Fisher and Thomas More

When sentence was passed, he spoke in the spirit of Christian charity referred to earlier. The scenes leading up to his execution are familiar. Going up to the scaffold – which was so weak that it was ready to fall – he said merrily to Master Lieutenant: 'I pray you, Master Lieutenant, see me safe up, and for my coming down, let me shift for myself.' In obedience to the King's command, he said little before execution, merely asking the people's prayers and protesting that he died in and for the Catholic faith. 'Afterwards, he exhorted them and earnestly beseeched them to pray God for the King, so that He would give him good counsel, protesting that he died his good servant, but God's first.'

We are not bound to admire the whole of More's life, although it has attracted many. His worldliness for much of the time seems far from holy, his attitude to heretics a good deal worse. But no-one who believes in sanctity at all, least of all the present writer, will question the rightness of his canonisation. One does not have to admire the whole life of a saint, St Augustine for example. The Church recognises that a flawed life can be rendered sublime by its final moments or, as in the case of St Augustine, and more briefly St Thomas More, its later stages. Thomas was a man much preoccupied with worldly considerations during most of his life, but totally purified well before the end.

10

ST IGNATIUS OF LOYOLA
1491–1556

St Ignatius of Loyola is known to all the world as the founder of the Jesuits. Lord Macauley's rhetorical passage concerning them is – or used to be – famous: 'With what vehemence, with what policy, with what exact discipline, with what dauntless courage, with what self-denial, with what forgetfulness of the dearest private ties, with what intense and stubborn devotion to a single end, with what unscrupulous laxity and versatility in the choice of means, the Jesuits fought the battle of their Church, is written in every page of the annals of Europe during several generations.' By any normal criterion, secular or spiritual, St Ignatius was one of the most successful men of action who ever lived. But he was also a supreme mystic, and no one ever combined the practical and the mystical more strikingly.

St Ignatius was probably born in 1491. His birth took place in the castle of Loyola. The youngest of twelve children, he came from one of the twenty-four families of the Basque nobility Guipuzcoas.

He was a young gallant, but his short military career came to an abrupt end on 20 May 1521. In the defence of Pamplona against the French a cannonball broke his right shin and tore open his left calf. He was captured, and sent in a litter to the castle of Loyola.

He himself in memoirs he dictated many years later described what followed, referring to himself throughout in the third person: 'He had set his mind on a worldly career, which he thought would not be helped by such a disfigurement' – that is, if one leg were shorter than the other. There was also an unsightly protuberance. 'He therefore enquired of the surgeons whether they would not cut away the bony projection. They replied that they undoubtedly could, but that the suffering entailed would be greater than any that he had hitherto borne, owing to the bone being healed and the operation necessarily a long one. Nevertheless he resolved to have his way and to undergo the martyrdom, though his elder brother marvelled and said that he himself would never be able to face such pain.'

Ignatius bore it all with composure. Having cut into the flesh and sawn off the projecting bone, the surgeons set themselves to increase the length of the leg, applying large quantities of unguents to it and continually stretching it by means of mechanical devices which, for several days on end, caused him terrible pain. But at last he began to feel very much better, except that he could not stand on the leg and was forced to remain lying on a couch.

While he was confined to his bed a book of the life of Christ and another containing the legends of the lives of the saints were brought to him. Again I turn to his own words: 'There was this difference between his reveries. When he was dwelling on worldly day-dreams, he found great delight in it, but when he abandoned them through weariness, he found himself arid and discontented. However, when he dreamed of going barefoot to Jerusalem, subsisting entirely on herbs and practising all other austerities which he saw the saints to have done, he was contented and joyful, not only in the presence of such thoughts, but remained so afterwards when they had gone.'

Desolation and consolation as criteria for establishing God's will had become realities for him. It also seemed to him that service to the greater honour of God consisted above all in doing penance. He gathered together sets of rules to help men to find a worthy way of life and began to formulate the spiritual exercises which were to become the inspiration of the Society of Jesus for many centuries.

By the end of February 1522 he was sufficiently cured to leave his paternal castle and from then on was dedicated to his new life. In March 1522 he arrived at the gates of the famous mountain monastery at Montserrat, at whose foot in Ignalada he provided himself with beggar's clothing, such as pilgrims usually wore. Bequeathing his mule to the monastery and giving away his elegant clothes, he donated his dagger and sword to the Black Madonna at Montserrat. After three days of preparation, Ignatius made a general confession to the pilgrims' father confessor, the Benedictine Juan Chanones. The night before the Feast of the Annunciation, 25 March 1522, he spent with the other pilgrims at the feet of the Madonna.

The morning after his vigil in Montserrat, he left the world of the monastery and went to Manresa, about five hours' journey away. For several months he stayed in Manresa, a ragged and ridiculed beggar. While living this mendicant life he suffered attacks of profound depression and inner despair. Thoughts of suicide were frequent. At the time he also underwent profound spiritual experiences, ones which supplied him with strength and inspiration for the rest of his life.

The most memorable of all his experiences occurred while he was walking along the banks of the river Cardona. 'Ignatius sat down, looking towards the water. While he sat there, the eyes of his understanding were opened. It was not a visual experience, but he was conscious of a comprehension, an intellectual revelation concerning spiritual matters that touch faith and Holy Writ, vivid beyond all comparison with what he had known or understood before, so that it all seemed quite new. His mind was so illuminated thereby that he seemed to himself to have become another man and to possess another understanding' (Henry Dwight Sidgwick).

So ended the first thirty-two years of his life. The last thirty-three fall into two parts almost equal in length. For fourteen years he travelled widely and seemed in retrospect to have been preparing himself for the last nineteen years of his life, which he spent in Rome. It did not seem like that at the time.

After staying in Manresa for about eighteen months, he started out on his longed-for pilgrimage to the Holy Land, arriving in Jerusalem by donkey. His firm intention was to stay there, but the Franciscan guardian of the holy places commanded him to leave Palestine, lest his attempts to convert Muslims should cause him to be kidnapped and held to ransom. His response was extraordinary. He returned to Spain and, aged thirty-three, noble but far from well-educated, sat down in a classroom with young boys and girls and set himself to study. By the time he was equipped to move to Paris (1528) he had already begun to gather round himself a small company. They gave catechism and instruction in the spiritual exercises. Both in Alcala and Salamanca, Ignatius ran into serious trouble with the authorities, was suspected of heresy, and was twice imprisoned.

For seven long years (1528–1535) he studied in Paris. From there he travelled in Spain and moved on to Venice, finally arriving in Rome in 1537, with two companions, Pierre Favre and Diego Lainez. In November 1537, about ten kilometres north of Rome, at the last mile post outside the city, Ignatius went into the little church of La Storta on the Via Cassia to pray. There he experienced a mystical enlightenment, similar to that he had known at Manresa, in which, as he describes it, he was profoundly moved by 'a conversion of his heart and soul with the three-fold God'. In this second 'vision' at La Storta he saw how God the Father joined him in Christ the Son, so that he could no longer have any doubts at all. It was Christ, poor, scorned, and carrying the cross to whom he now knew that he and his companions were united.

It was at that time that the proposal to form a religious order was conceived. Besides the vows of poverty, chastity and obedience it was resolved to add a fourth, and to appoint a Superior-General whom all in the Order should be bound to obey, subject entirely to the Holy See. Pope Paul III approved it by a Bull dated 27 September 1540. Ignatius was chosen as the first Superior-General, but only acquiesced in obedience to his confessor. As soon as the Society of Jesus is mentioned, the idea of discipline springs to mind. In recent years it has proved too big a strain for a number who have left the Society, but over the four hundred years since St Ignatius died and still today discipline has been the source of much of its strength.

He hardly left Rome during his remaining nineteen years, but he was ceaselessly active. On 15 May 1542 he took over the church of Santa Maria degli Astalli which contained the miraculous image of the Madonna della Strada. Alongside the church a simple new house was built where Ignatius lived from then on. Some 7,000 letters and instructions of his have been preserved, many of them extremely detailed. Through such letters he was able to stay in constant touch with his fellow brothers who had scattered to work throughout the world. Francis Xavier, for instance, was in India and Japan from 1540 onwards.

Ignatius continued to teach exercises, preach sermons and establish centres of charity in Rome. He had a house built near the Capitol for Moors and Jews who wanted to adopt the Christian faith. The Pope and many of the cardinals sought his advice. He worked constantly on the statutes of the Order, and ultimately a draft was unanimously agreed, though the final approval of the statutes did not take place until 1558, after his death, through the first General Congregation of the Society of Jesus.

In 1551 Ignatius asked his assembled brothers to transfer the guidance of the Order to someone else. Not surprisingly, in view of their profound respect for him, they refused. In his last years he suffered from a severe liver disorder. On the evening of 30 July 1556 he knew he was about to die. His secretary, however, did not want to send for the papal blessing for the dying until the next morning. Ignatius, the fighting man, capable of complete surrender, concurred with the words: 'Do as you will; I am totally in your hands.' He was heard praying softly at midnight: 'Oh my God.' He died without the last sacrament in the early hours of 31 July, at the age of sixty-five. He was beatified in 1609 by Pope Paul V and canonised in 1622 by Pope Gregory XV.

If one turns to St Ignatius's teaching one begins inevitably with the spiritual exercises. They have been well described as 'the chief means by which he imposed his vision and his will upon the young disciples'. He entertained an unshakeable assurance that what had proved of great succour and consolation to him would do as much for other sincere souls. He was convinced that there could be no better test of a man's fitness for a religious life than the manner in which he was affected by these exercises. Although undoubtedly he made alterations and additions at later times, he wrote the main part of the treatise at Manresa when he was just over thirty. The book is not meant to be put in the hands of a novice; it is a book of instruction for a spiritual director, full of suggestions as to how the message should be conveyed to the disciple and discipline imposed.

The exercises are intended for a period lasting about a month. A separate topic is dealt with each week. In the first, the novice follows the purgative way, and is bidden to fix his mind on the foulness of sin; during the following three weeks he is to contemplate the beauty of righteousness under varying conditions, in the person of Christ. There are two objects in view: first, the immediate, to inspire the heart with a desire for holiness, and to discipline it by means of the practices enjoined; second, the permanent, to improve the novice for all his life by teaching him to understand the true value of things.

All this, as we know, has proved enormously effective. At one point the Society of Jesus dominated Europe; it was suppressed in

1773 by the Pope, but it rose again and today is stronger than ever in Africa and South America. Whereas Lord Acton wrote of Saint Ignatius: 'He was that extraordinary man in whom the spirit of Catholic reaction is incorporated', the Jesuits at the present time tend to be regarded as a liberal force within the Church. The two Jesuits to whom I have owed more than I can express – Martin d'Arcy and Tom Corbishley – were totally unlike each other, though both men of exceptionally independent minds.

Countless books have been written in various languages about Ignatius. I myself have gained most in a short space from an essay by Karl Rahner, perhaps the most penetrating of Jesuit theologians in our period. Rahner (himself a Jesuit) puts himself in the position of Ignatius speaking to a modern Jesuit: 'As you know, my great desire was to "help souls", as I put it in my day; to tell people about God and his grace and about Jesus Christ, the Crucified and Risen, so that their freedom would become the freedom of God. I wanted to bring the same message as the Church had always brought and yet I felt, and with reason, that I could put the old message in new words. Why was this so? I was convinced that first, tentatively during my illness in Loyola and then, decisively, during my time as a hermit in Manresa, I had a direct encounter with God. This was the experience I longed to communicate to others.'

Rahner continues, still speaking as though he were St Ignatius today: 'When I claim to have known God at first hand, I do not intend here to add to my assertion a theological treatise on the nature of such a direct experience of God, nor a catalogue of all the accompanying phenomena of such an experience. All I say is I knew God, nameless and unfathomable, silent and yet near, bestowing himself upon me in his Trinity. I knew God beyond all concrete imaginings. I knew him clearly in such nearness and grace as is impossible to confound or mistake.'

I absolutely accept Rahner's contention that this consciousness of a direct encounter with God at Manresa lay at the heart of St Ignatius's message. God – 'really and truly, the God of incomprehensibility, the ineffable mystery, the darkness which only become eternal light for the man who allows himself to be swallowed up by it unconditionally. . .' .

There can be no doubt that the devotion of Ignatius's comrades, sustained over many years and beginning when his worldly prospects were negligible, was of unparalleled fervour. Yet he often treated some of them harshly, particularly Master Juan Pelanco, his secretary, who had been 'his hands and feet for nine years' unless it was the day before he died, when he sent him to ask for the Pope's blessing. And at times he gave Lainez (later his successor) such terrible scoldings (*dio tan terribles capellos*) that he made him cry: 'What makes it more singular still is, that our blessed Father said to me that there was no man in all the Society to whom it owed more than to Lainez, even including Father Xavier. . . . The year before he died, Ignatius behaved to him with great harshness . . . and Lainez felt so badly that he had recourse to the Lord and said: "Lord, what have I done against our Society that this saint treats me in this fashion?" '

That cry of Lainez is very revealing with its absolute recognition that Ignatius was indeed a saint. His followers loved him profoundly, putting up with treatment from him that they would not have done from any ordinary man because they were convinced that God spoke to them through Ignatius.

When the first General of the Order was being elected by the small group who had gathered round Ignatius, he himself, as mentioned above, was reluctant to accept the office, but agreed to do so under the guidance of his confessor. It is easy today to question the genuineness of such reluctance. In any human sense he must have known that he was the only possible choice, but he was at all times determined to maintain the tightest control on his human ego. He needed assurance on that point before he would give effect to the divine inspiration, to the almost continuous revelation that illuminated his soul concerning the Trinity, and the procession of the Holy Ghost from the Father and the Son.

If we look for his legacy we need only read the history of Europe and of other continents during the last four hundred years. But perhaps a quotation from his notebook leaves us with a truer impression of the man and the saint:

Saturday: fifth Mass of the Holy Trinity. At the usual prayers, nothing very much at the beginning; then, towards the middle of prayers, a sense of spiritual comfort, and the sight of something very resplendent. When the altar was being made ready, Jesus presented himself to my soul, and I felt moved to follow him, in the conviction that he is the chief and captain of the Company. . . .

Such words as these fit in well with the prayers most often associated with him:

Teach us, Lord
To serve you as you deserve,
To give and not to count the cost,
To fight and not to heed the wounds,
To labour and not to ask for reward
Save that of knowing that we do Your will,

Take, Lord, all my liberty
My memory, my understanding,
And my whole will.
You have given me all that I have,
All that I am,
And I surrender to Your Divine will.
That you dispose of me.
Give me only Your love and Your grace
With this I am rich enough
And I have no more to ask.

I have touched above on the almost unparalleled devotion to him of the members of his Order. His own absolute commitment to what he considered were their interests and that of the Society played a large part. But perhaps a memory supplied once more by Luis Goncalves offers a final reflection. Goncalves tells us that, in the last years, Ignatius would often say a prayer in his private chapel and sometimes Goncalves needed to consult him: 'Whenever I went in, and that was very often, his countenance shone, so that I stood still in amazement.'

A mystic, yes: a mystic who radiated joy.

I I

ST TERESA OF AVILA
1515–1582

St Teresa of Avila is beyond argument one of the most remarkable women who ever lived. The most potent of the many reasons for the vast extent of her appeal is no doubt her personality; but her extraordinary, if untutored, gift of writing has contributed to it largely. She is indeed accepted as one of the greatest writers of prose in the Spanish language. Her works have inspired many far advanced on the way of perfection, but they have also entered the homes of millions living in the world who know nothing of the contemplative life.

She was born in 1515. In 1537, she made her profession as a Carmelite nun. In 1562 she broke away and founded the first reformed Carmelite Convent. She founded many reformed convents thereafter. She died in 1582.

Before we come to her life and doctrine, a few words must be said about the personal impression she made on so many who knew her. Here the testimony of a non-Catholic and non-Christian writer of exceptional talent is as effective as any: 'That she was loved as well as feared,' wrote Vita Sackville-West in *The Eagle and the Dove*, 'is certain.' Teresa was evidently an exceptionally charming woman who inspired deep affection, which was sometimes sudden but always lasting; and apart from her qualities of saintliness, apart even from the liveliness of her mind and the fascination of her conversation, the magnet which drew this response was her own warm humanity. It was all very well for her to preach a fine detachment from worldy affections; she did not, she could not, live up to her own precepts in the least. St Teresa founded seventeen convents in less than twenty years, at times contending with the most complicated difficulties (and frenzied opposition). She was concerned in the foundation of a number of monasteries, she undertook long, fatiguing and often dangerous journeys all over Spain, she wrote a number of books. She suffered from interruption through constant illness, yet the letters continued to pour from her in a torrent: intimate, affectionate, upbraiding, practical, dashing from subject to subject, breathless. Her rare spiritual power expressed itself in countless human relations during her lifetime and has communicated itself ever more widely as the centuries pass. I have described St Francis of Assisi as the best-loved of all the saints but St Teresa, a totally different character, runs him close.

. She came of a well-to-do and cultured family. Her father's father was a Jewish convert to Catholicism, who was treated at one point in a most humiliating fashion by representatives of the Inquisition. They had, round about 1480, begun to root out all so-called New Christians – converts to the Catholic Church and their descendants suspected of 'Judaizing', that is reverting to their ancestral faith or secretly continuing its practices. It is said that Teresa's grandfather was made to wear a 'garment of shame', a yellow tunic with large green crosses at the back and front, taking his place in a penitential procession. This same grandfather showed exceptional resilience and enterprise in rebuilding both his fortune and his reputation. The family moved from Toledo to Avila, where a close relation was carrying on a flourishing trade in silk and woollen cloth. Advantageous marriages followed. Teresa's father married the well-born Caroline del Peso y Henao. She died leaving two children. Later Don Alonso, as he was now called, married Doña Beatriz de Ahumada, once again from a family of repute. More children were born, including Teresa.

Doña Beatriz was deeply religious. However, worn out by illness and constant confinements, she died early, when Teresa was thirteen. At sixteen, Teresa attempted to become a nun, but she fell ill and had to be sent home. Her resolution was only temporarily tested. In 1536, when twenty-one, she left home once more to become a novice at the Convent of the Incarnation. The following year she made her profession as a Carmelite nun, but again illness overtook her and for a time she left the convent. When she returned in April 1539, she fell ill once more, this time desperately so. On the night of 15 August, she suffered a prolonged fit which seems to have been cataleptic. Confronted with so alarming a phenomenon, sixteenth-century medical skill was powerless. The young nun was pronounced dead – indeed, in one of those graphic touches which so enliven her autobiography she tells us that when she eventually recovered consciousness she found wax on her eyelids. A grave was dug for her in the convent grounds and, for a day and a half, the sisters awaited her dead body. By the mercy of God, however, she escaped being buried alive, and at the end of four days came to herself again. Here is her own vivid account of her 'intolerable sufferings':

> My tongue was bitten to pieces; nothing had passed my lips; and because of this and my great weakness my throat was choking me so that I could not even take water. All my bones seemed to be out of joint and there was a terrible confusion in my head . . . . I could move, I think, only one finger of my right hand . . . . They used to move me in a sheet, one taking one end and another the other.

To counter-balance these physical trials, Teresa had been enjoying spiritual experiences which were the foundation of many more to come.

Chronology in her case is more than usually difficult, but it is essential in studying her life, particularly her early years as a nun, to realise the terror that the figure of the Devil exercised. The Devil, his personal appearance, and his wiles were very real to her. She speaks of his intrigues as of a mischievous person she might have known in the world, almost in a matter-of-fact, taken-for-granted way; his mischief was to do all in his power to steal souls from God, with such subtlety and ingenuity that it was necessary to be continually on one's guard. Sometimes he appeared in extraordinary guise: 'he appeared multiplied, as when she saw the dead body in a winding sheet, tossed to and fro by devils, who also dragged it about with great hooks . . . . In Hell it is the soul itself that tears itself in pieces with an inward fire surpassing all torments and all pain. . . . The terror of that vision was so greatly upon her, as she set it down on paper six years later, that the natural warmth of her body was chilled even as she wrote.'

It is difficult to know where precisely to date the beginning of Teresa's mystical life. Stephen Clissold, in his excellent *Centuries of Avila*, allocated it to 1554. His chronology runs:

1554 A vision of the wounded Christ marks the beginning of Teresa's mystical life.
1556 She experiences the 'Mystical Betrothal'.
1557 Her friends pronounce her possessed.

As regards Teresa's visions, we can again fall back on the cool but sympathetic appraisal of Vita Sackville-West. These were to Teresa 'a source of mingled worry and joy. At long last she came to accept them as the true appearance of the divine presence, but even then her analytical mind continued to ferret after the explanation of their exact nature'. Vita Sackville-West sets out to examine what Teresa has to say of this extraordinary interior life 'which doubled her active and practical existence'. She was utterly convinced of the reality of her experience. To quote Teresa's words: 'These ecstasies come upon me with great violence and in such a way as to be outwardly visible, I having no power to resist them, even when I am with others, for they come in such a way as to admit of no disguising them unless it be by letting people suppose that, as I am subject to disease of the heart, they are fainting fits. I take great pains to resist them when they are coming on – sometimes I cannot do it.'

For the moment, I am concerned with Teresa's visions as part of her life. Their significance as part of her doctrine or message or mystical philosophy I will turn to later. It seems that the first project for the reform of the Carmelite Order was suggested to Teresa when she was forty-three, when she had been twenty-two years at the Convent of the Incarnation. During those years she was, on the face of it, an ordinary nun, but it would seem that she had already made a deep impression on all who met her, and the news of her ecstasies was already current.

One day in 1559 (?), after communion, she received a command from God which altered her life. Professor Allison Peers, the leading authority on Teresa, treats this as the turning-point. 'For by this time she had trained herself not only to follow her superiors, but to listen for, and obey the voice of God. And there could be no mistake about what she heard now: the Lord made her wonderful promises and gave her "the most explicit commands" to work for them with all her might. He even gave the convent-to-be the name by which it was to become famous – St Joseph's – and ended by charging Teresa to tell her confessor this, and to say "that it was He who was giving her this command and that He asked him not to oppose it or to hinder her in carrying it out".'

She had to deal with a whole host of religious authorities who, of course, changed in personnel over the twenty-five years she was arguing with them. There was always her confessor; there was the

Provincial of her Order; there was the Vicar-General; there was the representative of the Pope; there were various Jesuit friends and, not to be ignored even in religious matters, the King of Spain. She would have been inhuman and extremely foolish not to have attempted at all times to find the authorities who suited her purpose best. But one must remember that she was conscious that the supreme command came to her from above. In her writings she always treated humility as the supreme virtue. The messages she received were in no sense hers. When she described herself as a worthless person, she meant it. The messages were sacred. Nevertheless she was utterly loyal to the Catholic Church at all times and if there was a big tension in her life it was the effort frequently required to find a way of reconciling the messages from above with Catholic authority.

We must understand the reasons for her indomitable determination to initiate a reform of the Carmelite Order. She became convinced, much encouraged by her 'voices', that there must be an immediate return to the primitive austerities of Mount Carmel, or at least to the strict observance of the Carmelite rule as it existed before the 1440 Bill of Mitigation. An end to laxity! Not unexpectedly among the nuns of the Convent of the Incarnation there was a strong resistance. The last change they wanted was to have their pleasant way of life disturbed.

To quote the *Life*:

> The nuns said that I was insulting them; that there were others there who were better than myself, and so I could serve God quite well where I was; that I had no love for my own convent; and that I should have done better to get money for that than for founding another. Some said I ought to be thrown into the prison cell.

The clamour and hostility were vehement and prolonged. A house had been found and the deeds were ready for signature. The Provincial went back on his promise and refused his consent. Teresa in turn refused to accept any idea of endowment, and this led to still further criticism. Through it all she remained serene and indeed laughed heartily about the suggestion that she might be denounced to the Inquisition:

> I told them not to be afraid, for my soul would be in a very bad way if there were anything about it which could make me fear the Inquisition.

If ever I thought there might be, I would go and pay a visit of my own accord; and if anything were alleged against me the Lord would deliver me and I should be very much the gainer.

Teresa found allies where she could. The new Jesuit rector of Avalon House became her director and gave her unqualified support in her plans for reform. In August 1561, after collecting some money from various sources, 'she arranged for her own sister, Doña Juana de Ahumada, to buy and furnish a house for a convent whose numbers would be limited to thirteen.' Why should it need any money of its own? Why should it not trust to God for its income? The bishop was talked over. This first foundation was made on St Bartholomew's day 24 August 1562.

The commotion broke out again with renewed fury. The city council and the Cathedral chapter demanded that the house be closed but Teresa never wavered. The dispute dragged on from August 1562 to August 1564, but on 22 August the provisional permission of the Provincial was made official. A year later it was confirmed by the Papal Nuncio. She was secure at last, and with her the whole dream of reforming and purifying the Carmelite Order.

The steady progress at St Joseph's was very satisfying, but the most famous step she took was the writing of her *Life* which she completed in 1562. F. C. Happold, in his book *Mysticism*, describes the *Life* as 'one of the most charmingly intimate and self-revealing spiritual autobiographies ever written'. Here I can only pick out one famous section about the degrees of prayer:

A beginner must look on himself as one setting out to make a garden for his Lord's pleasure . . . . Let us see how this garden is to be watered. It seems to me that the garden may be watered in four different ways. Either the water must be drawn from a well, which is very laborious; or by a water-wheel and buckets, worked by a windlass. I have sometimes drawn it in this way, which is less laborious than the other and brings up more water – or from a stream or spring, which waters the ground much better, for the soil then retains more moisture and needs watering less often, which entails far less work for the gardener; or by heavy rain, when the Lord waters it Himself without any labour of ours; and this is an incomparably better method than all the rest.

She then proceeds to apply these four methods of watering to the four degrees of prayer. Beginners in prayer are those who draw the water up out of the well which, she emphasises, is 'a great labour'. This drawing of water means, to use her expression, 'working with understanding'.

The second degree of prayer – the water-wheel – represents that state of recollection called the Prayer of Quiet. The understanding which has laboured so hard in the first degree is now at rest and with it the memory; only the will is active, but it 'allows itself to be imprisoned by God, as one who well knows itself to be the captive of Him whom it loves.'

In the third degree, in which the garden is watered by a river or spring, 'God may almost be said to be the gardener Himself, for it is He who does everything.' To the world this state is folly and madness – but 'it is a glorious folly, a heavenly madness, in which true wisdom is acquired, and a mode of fruition in which the soul finds its greatest delight.'

In the fourth degree all the faculties are united with God. The soul seems to be 'fainting almost completely away, in a kind of swoon, with an exceeding great and sweet delight.' Not infrequently supernatural phenomena reveal themselves, such as rapture, elevation and flight of the spirit. At all times the soul 'feels close to God and there abides within it such a certainty that it cannot do other than believe.'

One might feel that, with the possible exception of her younger friend, St John of the Cross, no one has carried us further into the realms of mysticism than St Teresa in her *Life*; but by common consent Teresa was to go deeper still.

From 1565, at the earnest request of the nuns of the first convent of the reform, that is, St Joseph's, she was writing *The Way of Perfection*. She never wrote more tersely or more effectively. Her message is one of daring and defiance, the very essence of the counter-reformation. 'We cannot be forced to surrender by hunger; we can die, but we cannot be conquered.' Allison Peers sums up one outstanding aspect: 'Teresa had set her face like a flint and it is for its flint-like qualities that *The Way of Perfection* will always be known.'

In 1567 occurred a turning-point on the worldly plane as decisive as the message received from God in 1559 endorsing her idea of founding a reformed convent. St Joseph's was visited by the Vicar-General of the Carmelite Order. His visit was awaited with trepidation, but he whole-heartedly approved the reform. Later he was to prove much less supportive. However, at the time he told Teresa that he was anxious for further experiments of the same kind and gave her patents for the foundation of more convents in such a way as to over-ride the possible objection of any future Provincial. Her whole horizon was transformed. She needed no further encouragement. Between 1567 and 1582 she founded altogether sixteen convents in accordance with her reformed ideas. She ran into appalling difficulties but her achievements multiplied.

> Have no misgivings as to how I shall govern you, for though I have thus far lived among and governed nuns who are Discalced, I know well, through the Lord's goodness, the way to govern those who are not. My desire is that we should all serve the Lord in quietness and do the little which our Rule and Constitutions command us for the love of that Lord. . . .

She presided over St Joseph's for the regulation three years. For the last two of these, her friendship with St John of the Cross inspired them both equally.

From 1575 to 1579 she was engaged in almost ceaseless conflict with one or more of the authorities mentioned earlier. In 1575 the Vicar-General who had supplied the original encouragement disapproved of the reform on the grounds that Teresa had moved far outside the area originally discussed.

In 1577 St John of the Cross was abducted by hostile friars, the so-called 'Calced' or unreformed. The dispute between the Calced and Discalced (or reformed) reached its height in 1578. In 1579, Teresa was at last permitted to resume her travels. Meanwhile, while things were at their worst, in 1577, she wrote what is often considered the most profound of her books: *The Interior Castle*.

Here one can only offer a few extracts. On Trinity Eve, 1 June 1577, the ideas suddenly crystallised into a vivid picture: a most beautiful crystal globe, made in the shape of a castle, and containing seven mansions, in the seventh and innermost of which was the King of Glory, in the greatest splendour, illumining and beautifying them all:

> The nearer one got to the centre, the stronger was the light; outside the palace limits everything was foul, dark and infested with toads, vipers and other venomous creatures. While she was wondering at the

beauty, which by God's grace can dwell in the human soul, the light suddenly vanished. Although the King of Glory did not leave the mansions, the crystal globe was plunged into darkness, became as black as coal and emitted an insufferable odour, and the venomous creatures outside the palace boundaries were permitted to enter the castle.

The next day she sat down to write and completed the book at record speed. The mystic way is represented by the progress in the outer courtyard of the castle 'where the most secret things pass between God and the soul'. The castle itself is the soul, but, in the words of Allison Peers, 'that seeming paradox presents no difficulty for the Kingdom of God is within you'.

The first mansion is that of humility; the second that of the practice of prayer; the third of meditation and exemplary life. In the terms of the *Life*, the first three of the mansions correspond to · the first water; in the fourth mansion, corresponding to the second water, the pilgrim gains the gift of God which is known as the Prayer of Quiet. The fifth mansion, corresponding with slight variations to the third water is commonly known as the Prayer of Union or the Spiritual Betrothal. It has been made famous by her metaphor of the silkworm – when the worm which was large and ugly 'comes right out of the cocoon a beautiful white butterfly'. The silkworm is of course the contemplative soul:

> By comparison with the abode it has had, everything it sees on earth leaves it dissatisfied. . . . It sets no store by the things it did when it was a worm. . . . It has wings now. . . . All that it can do for God seems to it slight by comparison with its desires. . . . Everything else wearies it, because it has proved that it can find no true rest in the creatures.

The sixth mansion is described as a 'kind of incipient union' characterised by greater afflictions and corresponding in some sort with St John of the Cross's 'dark night of the spirit'. In the seventh mansion we are led into the innermost chamber of the King. The pilgrim is led into it by an intellectual vision in which all three persons of the Trinity reveal themselves.

In the *Life* the fourth water was an experience of brief duration, but the seventh mansion, the Marriage, is for ever and ever. With only the briefest intervals the Marriage is a state of permanent peace. Teresa wrote in 1581: 'My acts and desires seem not to be as strong as they once were. I have a desire much more powerful than any of them – that the will of God may be done.' Now habitually she longed neither for death nor for life. Only one state could be higher – that of the beatific vision of the life to come.

In 1580 it was at last agreed that the Calced and the Discalced orders should be separated. Teresa, failing in health, worked to the last, founding four more convents before her death at Alba de Tormes on 4 October 1582. She was canonised forty years later by Pope Gregory XV. The pursuit of her relics is pretty gruesome by modern standards, but nothing of that kind can affect her greatness or sanctity.

One cannot help comparing her life with that of St Ignatius of Loyola, born twenty-four years earlier, like herself a Spaniard and supreme mystic. She said of herself: 'When I was nearly forty, from then on I turned over a new leaf and led another life. Until then it was a matter of my own life for myself; thenceforward it was God's life in me.' That could well have come from St Ignatius. The society he founded, the Jesuits, has been of much greater significance in the world than the reformed Carmelites; but St Teresa was a much superior writer. We share her spirit much more easily than his.

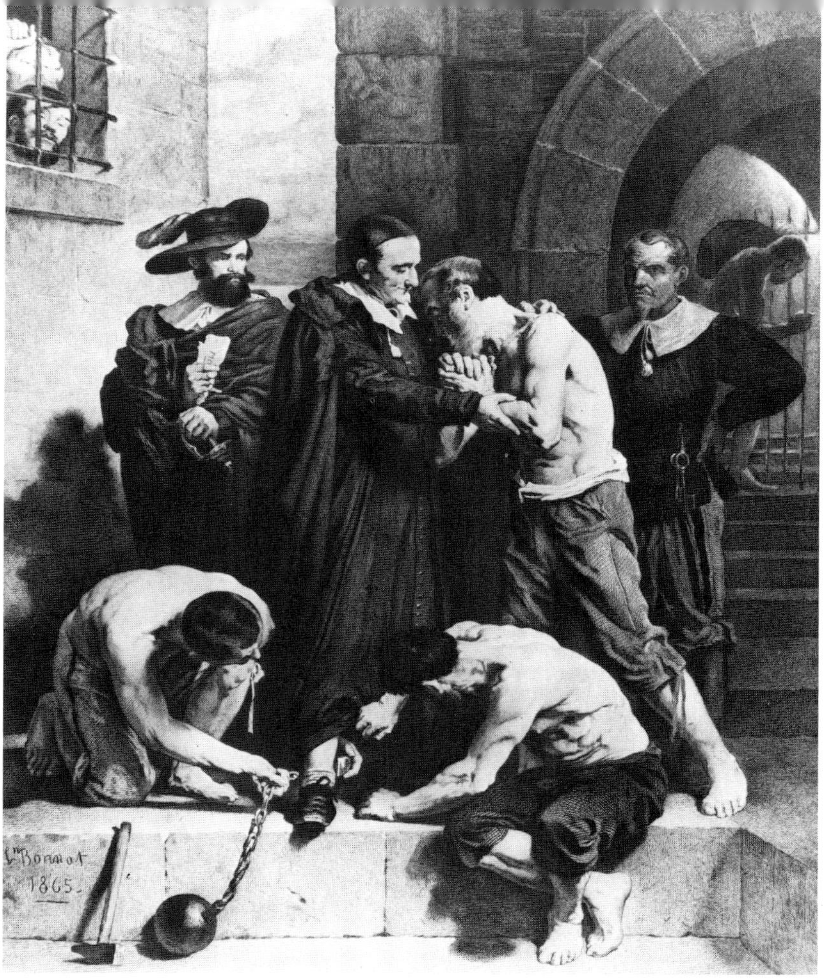

ABOVE:
St. Vincent de Paul (1581–1660)

RIGHT:
St. Theresa of Lisieux (1873–1897)
with her mother

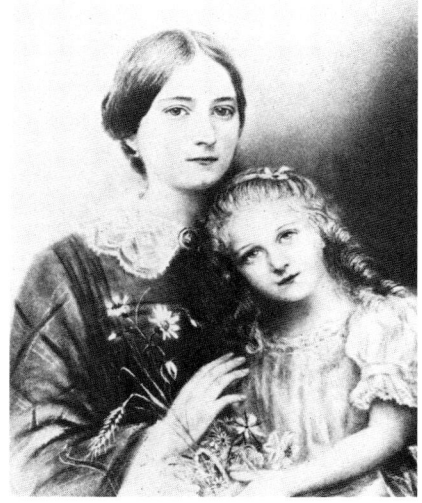

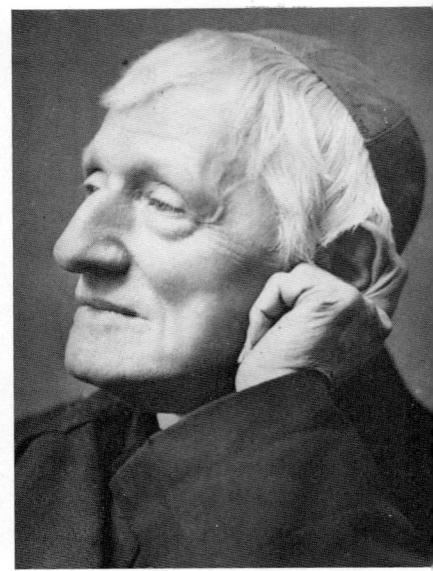

The 'almost Saints'

ABOVE LEFT:
Martin Luther (1483–1546)

ABOVE:
Cardinal Newman (1801–1890)

LEFT:
Archbishop Temple (1881–1944)

FACING PAGE, ABOVE RIGHT:
Fr. Maximilian Kolbe, the Polish priest who gave up his life for a Polish inmate at Auschwitz

FACING PAGE, ABOVE FAR RIGHT:
Martin Luther King, assassinated in 1968

ABOVE:
Oscar Romero, Archbishop of San
Salvador, who was murdered in
March 1980

RIGHT:
Pope John Paul II sits beneath a
picture of Karolina Kozka, who was
killed in 1914 by Russian soldiers.
She was beatified in June 1987

Two modern writers
exercised by the idea of
sanctity:

ABOVE:
T.S. Eliot discusses with
actor Robert Speight his
play *Murder in the
Cathedral*

RIGHT:
Graham Greene, creator
of the whisky priest of
The Power and the Glory

12

ST JOHN OF THE CROSS
1542–1591

St John of the Cross is, by common consent, the mystic's mystic. Among our selected saints he is also the only eminent poet. In that respect he stands on the same footing in Spanish literature as Saint Teresa does as a writer of prose.

The life of such a supreme contemplative might be expected to be one of peace and quiet – at least, in a worldly sense. In fact John was engaged for a number of years in varied activities. Twice at least he was subjected to very painful treatment.

He was born at Fontiveros, in Old Castile, in 1542 and was to die in 1591, aged just under fifty. His father belonged to a good Toledan family but, having married beneath him, was disinherited and had to earn his living as a silk weaver. On his death his wife was left destitute and with three children, of whom John was the youngest. He went to a poor school at Medina del Campo and was later apprenticed to a weaver, but he showed no aptitude for the trade and was taken on as a servant by the governor of the hospital at Medina. He stayed there for seven years, already practising bodily austerities, and continuing his studies in the college of the Jesuits. At twenty-one he took the religious habit among the Carmelite friars at Medina, receiving the name of John-of-St-Matthias. In 1567, aged twenty-five, he was ordained a priest.

At this time St Teresa of Avila was deeply involved in the reformation of the Carmelites. She met St John at Medina and told him that she had received authority from the Prior General to found two reformed houses of men. She liked what she had heard of his spirit and had selected him to be an early instrument of the work. A beginning was made at Duruelo. The fame of the sanctity of this secure house spread, and three other houses were soon established. Then in 1571 St Teresa undertook the office of prioress of the unreformed Convent of the Incarnation at Avila. She sent for St John to be its spiritual director and confessor.

No spiritual association could have been more fruitful, but Teresa's period of office ended in 1574. This was the period when violent disputes were breaking out between the reformed and the unreformed Carmelites. At length, in 1577, the Provincial of Castile ordered St John to return to his original friary at Medina. He refused, on the grounds that he held his office from the Papal Nuncio. Armed men were sent who carried him off to Toledo, where he was locked up in a small cell, ten feet by six, with practically no light. He was repeatedly beaten and bore the marks to his dying day. His immediate answer was his earliest poem.

After nine months he made his escape, fleeing to the reformed priory of Beas de Segura and then to the nearby hermitage of Monte Calvario. In 1579 he became head of the college at Baeza and in 1581 was chosen Prior of Los Martines near Granada. He became Vicar for Andalusia and founded more priories: not only in a spiritual sense, he had become a leading figure in the Order. He also took an active share in the manual labour involved when monasteries were in the course of erection, joining the workmen, while the nuns often benefited from his work in the garden. Sweeping and scrubbing or other tasks of ordinary life were never shirked by him.

However, it was as a spiritual director that he came into his own. As a true physician of souls, he tried to free people from any sickness or imperfection which prevented them from flying to union with God. He concentrated on the interior rather than on the exterior and, in fact, contrary to the image often portrayed, was inclined to moderate external penances. He was obviously aware of sado-masochism when he referred in his writings to the 'penance of beasts'.

Life became hard for him, however, when Nicholas Doria was made Vicar-General. He reduced St John from all offices to the status of a simple friar, packed him off to a remote friary at Penuela then later gave him the choice of going either to Baeza or Ubeda. St John chose the latter as presenting on the face of it the more unpleasant prospect, the Prior there being someone whom he had himself corrected at an earlier point. This Prior treated him with much inhumanity, but St John was by now very sick. He died, still under an official cloud, although the Prior repented at the eleventh hour of his behaviour and was forgiven by St John.

The proposition that all saints have been lovable is highly

debatable, but not in the case of St John. Allison Peers sums up the outstanding impression made by him as that of a man of God. He was 'so *good* a man' reported St Teresa after her first long period of contact with him. *Harto Santo* – 'a real saint' was her verdict after she had experienced him as confessor. And the word *santo* used either as a noun or in its adjectival sense of 'saintly' is continually applied to him elsewhere. 'For myself during the whole time I knew him,' declared a friar some twenty years after St John's death, 'I saw a simple, sincere, unaffected sanctity.'

St Teresa summed up the effect which he produced upon others without mincing her language. 'They take him for a saint,' she wrote, 'and a saint in my opinion he is, and has been all his life.'

It is of course through his writings that St John has come to be so widely admired. He left behind three treatises: *The Ascent of Mount Carmel – The Dark Night*, *The Spiritual Canticle* and *The Living Flame of Love* (*The Dark Night* is best seen as a continuation of *The Ascent of Mount Carmel*). Each of these three treatises was preceded by a poem of which the treatise was indeed to be regarded as an elucidation and expansion.

St John wrote a number of other poems, and is regarded by good judges as one of the finest poets in the Spanish language. In this respect at least there is no other saint who compares with him, though a number have surpassed him as prose stylists. A famous tribute was paid to St John's poetry in an address on mystical poetry to the Spanish Academy by Memendez y Pelayo: 'So sublime is this poetry that it scarcely seems to belong to this world at all; it is hardly capable of being assessed by literary criteria. More ardent in its passion than any profane poetry, its form is elegant and exquisite, as plastic and highly figured as any of the finest works of the Renaissance. The spirit of God has passed through these poems every one, beautifying and sanctifying them on its way.'

It seems to be accepted that his earlier writing is no different in thought from his later. The themes with which he deals are also constant; the way leading to union with God and a life itself of divine union. It is not therefore of the first importance to decide exactly when the serious treatises and poems were written. All the works that have come down to us were, however, written during the last fourteen years of his life between the ages of thirty-six and forty-nine. It is impossible to convey even a glimmering of the character of St John without a few quotations from his poems. That which serves as a starting point for *The Ascent of Mount Carmel* and *The Dark Night* begins with the famous stanzas:

> One dark night
> Fired with love's urgent longings
> – Ah, the sheer grace! –
> I went out unseen.
> My house being now all stilled.
>
> In darkness and secure,
> By the secret ladder disguised,
> – Ah, the sheer grace! –
> In darkness and concealment,
> My house being now all stilled. . . .

It concludes:

> When the breeze blew from the turret
> Parting His hair
> He wounded my neck
> With His gentle hand,
> Suspended all my senses
> I abandoned and forgot myself
> Laying my face on my Beloved;
> All things ceased, I went out from myself
> Leaving my cares
> Forgotten among the lilies.

On the opening page of *The Ascent of Mount Carmel* St John indicates the nature of his treatise by declaring his intention to explain how one reaches 'the highest state of perfection'. It is a work which describes the path to be followed in order to reach perfection, which he identifies as union with God. The poetic figure Dark Night provides St John with a metaphor to indicate the entire way which leads to union with God. In passing from the initial stages of the spiritual life to perfect union with God, the soul must leave all things by denying its appetite for them and advance by means of truth to God, its end. Creatures in themselves do not thwart union with God; it is the voluntary inordinate appetite that interferes with this union. In the active night of the senses, a person must struggle particularly for the habit of seeking only God's honour and glory. In the passive night of the senses God communicates a general and obscure knowledge –

'contemplation which is imparted through faith'. In expounding the passive night of the spirit St John explores still more fully the manner in which God purifies the soul.

In the *Spiritual Canticle*, he tells of the loving exchange which takes place between the soul and Christ, its bridegroom. The poem in this case is very much longer. A brief quotation does it less than justice:

Bride: Where have you hidden
         Beloved, and left me moaning?
         You fled like the stag
         After wounding me;
         I went out calling You, and You were gone.

Bridegroom:
         The small white dove
         Has returned to the ark with an olive branch
         And now the turtle dove
         Has found its longed-for mate
         By the green river banks.

Bride: There you will show me
         What my soul has been seeking.
         And then You will give me,
         You, my life, will give me there
         What you gave me on that other day.

In understanding the whole poem, I have been much helped by Keiran Kavanagh, editor of St John's collected works. We begin with a person's initial steps in the service of God. Eventually he reaches spiritual marriage, the ultimate stage of perfection. The poem refers therefore to the three states, purgative, illuminative and unitive, through which a person passes on his way to the goal, and explains their significance.

The Living Flame of Love carries the message of *The Spiritual Canticle* to a still more profound level. St John writes in the prologue to *The Living Flame*: 'Although in the stanzas we have already commented on, we speak of the highest degree of perfection one can reach in this life (transformation in God) these stanzas treat of a love within this very state of transformation that has a deeper quality and is more perfect.' The poem in this case is much shorter than *The Spiritual Canticle*, only four stanzas in fact, of which I will quote two:

O living flame of love
That tenderly wounds my soul
In its deepest centre! since
Now you are not oppressive,
Now consummate! if it be Your will:
Tear through the veil of this sweet encounter!

How gently and lovingly
You wake in my heart,
Where in secret You dwell alone;
And in your sweet breathing,
Filled with good and glory
How tenderly you swell my heart with love.

What of the saint's message? 'St John,' says Fr Martin d'Arcy, SJ, 'explains how, with the grace of God, those who are drawn to contemplation experience the presence of God in a way comparable to that we enjoy when our friends meet us. The way, however, is exceedingly arduous, so arduous in fact as to terrify all except the bravest of lovers.' It comes to this, that we must surrender all that is dearest to us in the enjoyment of the senses and go through a dark night in which we live without their help and comfort. D'Arcy continues: 'Then when this is accomplished, we have to sacrifice the prerogative of our own way of thinking and willing and undergo another still darker night in which we have deprived ourselves of all the supports which are familiar to us and make us self-sufficient. This is a kind of death, the making nothing of all that we are to ourselves; but the genuine mystic tells us that, when all has been strained away, our emptiness will be filled with a new presence; our uncovered soul will receive the contact of divine love, and a new circuit of love will begin, when the soul is passive to an indescribable love which is given to it.'

Allison Peers, in his short but classic book *The Spirit of Flame*, has two illuminating chapters called 'Stumbling Blocks (1) and (2)'. He puts himself in the position of the plain man coming to the works of St John and finding himself far from enchanted. 'When his eyes have at last grown accustomed to the blackness of this new world and he begins to distinguish its outlines more clearly, the most outstanding feature causes him a positive repulsion. This is the Saint's teaching on detachment.' The plain man concludes that detachment in St John's sense must mean the complete annihilation of every natural desire, not only detachment from sensual and exterior things for the saint also prescribes detachment from the spiritual. 'The soul must not only be disencumbered from that which belongs to the creatures, but likewise as it travels, it must be annihilated from all that belongs to the spirit.' Allison Peers insists that one way of defending St John is to point to his love of music and of nature. It is not *all* appetite nor *all* creatures that thwart union with God. It is the voluntary *inordinate* (my italics) appetites that stand in the way. In the unfinished third book of *The Ascent of Mount Carmel*, St John lays down 'a test' by which we may know when pleasures of sense are profitable and when they are not. 'It is that, whenever a person hears music and other things and sees pleasant things and is conscious of sweet perfumes . . . if his thought and the affection of his will are at once centred upon God and if that thought of God gives him more pleasure than the movement of sense which causes it, this is a sign that he is receiving benefit therefrom and that this thing of sense is a help to his experience.'

St John of the Cross has inspired countless readers with spiritual ambitions, even though they recognise the hard truth that one cannot share the mystic's ideal without sharing the mystic's sacrifice. The question remains: what does he say to me? To that question there will be many different answers. A very spiritual woman, who has been through much turmoil and who is now an exclaustrated nun, writes to me: 'I am aware of a real communion with him. I can say without exaggeration that often when I reach sinking point, his words, when I open his works, seem to stabilise me once more in God.' She insists that it is incorrect to say, with one or two writers: 'He taught all or nothing. One should say rather: He taught all *and* nothing. If one aims at the ALL-thing, one must desire NO-thing. To reach satisfaction in ALL-thing, desire its possession in NO-thing.'

That, at certain moments, I think I begin to understand.

13
ST FRANCIS DE SALES
1567–1622

In the encyclical of January 1923, Pope Pius XI commended St Francis de Sales as 'the spiritual writer perhaps the most suited of all to meet the religious needs of the world at the present day'. That is still a convincing verdict. The Pope declared *The Introduction to the Devout Life* to be the most perfect book of its kind, and described the treatise *On the Love of God* as of still greater moment and importance. For my part if I were allowed to take only one book other than the Bible to a desert island, I would choose *The Introduction to the Devout Life*. Francis de Sales therefore will continue to appeal to countless spiritual seekers throughout the world through his writings. In addition to his books, he wrote innumerable letters, the most famous being those to Saint Jeanne-Françoise Chantal, a founder with him of the Visitation Order of Nuns.

His life, even apart from his writings, was immensely edifying. He was born at the Château de Sales in Savoie on 21 August 1567. His patron saint in later life was the Poverello of Assisi (St Francis). During his first years he was very frail and delicate owing to his premature birth. He gradually grew stronger, however, and throughout his career he was singularly active and energetic. He died nevertheless at the early age of fifty-five.

At the age of eight he went to the College of Annecy. A year later he received the tonsure. He had already a great wish to consecrate himself to God. His father, however, destined him – the eldest son – for a secular career. In his fourteenth year he was sent to the University of Paris, later persuading his father to allow him to go to the College de Clermont, which was under Jesuit direction and renowned for piety as well as for learning. To satisfy his father, he took lessons in riding, dancing and fencing, but 'cared for none of them' (Butler's *Lives of the Saints*). By the time he was twenty-four, he was not only highly trained in theology, but had become a doctor of law at Padua.

Eventually, overcoming the resistance of his father, he was ordained a priest on 18 December 1593. He was soon despatched to the Chablais, a Calvinist stronghold, though the people of the district had recently become subjects of the Catholic Duke of Savoy. Francis later described to the Pope the appalling prospect which had greeted him and his cousin Louis: 'Nothing but heart-breaking sights met our eyes. Out of sixty-five parishes, excepting for a few officers of the Duke's garrisons, thee were scarcely fifty Catholics. The churches were desecrated or destroyed, and the cross everywhere broken down.'

Francis and his cousin were exposed to much danger. Fanatical Calvinists had sworn to kill them and made several attempts to do so. But the *Every Man's Book of Saints* [which follows the calendar of the *Alternative Service Book*] generously describes the success of his labours: 'His courage, endurance and gentleness spoke forcibly to the presence of the Chablais. Conversions became frequent and lapsed Catholics sought reconciliation with their Church in ever-increasing numbers.'

In 1598 the Chablais ceased officially to be Protestant. In 1599 Saint Francis was appointed Coadjutor Bishop of Geneva. In 1602 he went to Paris and preached a course of sermons in the Chapel Royal. Henry IV offered him every inducement to remain in Paris, but Francis made the famous reply: 'I have married a poor bride and I cannot forsake her for a richer.' In the same year he succeeded to the See of Geneva.

He became famous and indeed criticised for the apparent leniency of his doctrine. But he was always severe on himself, though he never went to extremes of penance. He gave away his private fortune saying: 'When one has but little, one has little to give, little to answer for. No one is really poor who has enough to live on. Had it been the will of God I would rather have been a humble priest, carrying holy water and tending a few poor people, than wear the mitre and staff.'

We are told in Butler's *Lives of the Saints* that 'children loved him and followed him about. His unselfishness and charity, his humility and clemency, could not have been surpassed. In dealing with souls, though always gentle, he was never weak, and he could be very firm when kindness did not prevail.'

His dearest friend and fellow saint-to-be was Jeanne-Françoise Chantal. She first became known to him in 1604, when he was preaching Lenten sermons at Dijon. The foundation of the Order of Visitation in 1610 was the outcome.

His most famous book, *The Introduction to the Devout Life*, grew out of the casual notes of instruction and advice which he wrote to Madame de Chamoisy, a cousin by marriage, who had placed herself under his guidance. He was persuaded to publish them in a little volume which, with some additions, first appeared in 1608. The book was at once acclaimed a spiritual masterpiece, and soon translated into many languages.

In 1616, he published his book *Treatise on the Love of God*, a much more systematic treatise than the *Introduction* and intended to carry the search for God on to a higher plane. Dr Michael Muller, in his book about the spiritual theology of Saint Francis, has this to say of the two books: 'In its wealth and depth of thought this book stands higher than the *Introduction* – too high in fact for the mass of people who for all that, and in spite of its length, read it with enthusiasm, but were not in a position to understand completely the philosophy of the Love of God or to integrate it into the daily conduct of their lives. Hence the *Love of God* became the guidebook of those with a mystical tendency while the *Introduction* became a popular book which everybody could understand and which at the same time remained entirely satisfying to the informed.'

He was offered the office of Coadjutor Bishop of Paris with the right of succession, after undertaking a mission in that city in 1618. But he refused, saying: 'One does not give oneself to the Church in order to secure a position, but to till that piece of ground allotted to the householder.'

In 1622 the Duke of Savoy, going to meet Louis XIII at Avignon, invited Francis to join them there. Anxious to obtain from Louis certain privileges for the French part of his diocese, Francis readily consented, 'although he was in no state of health to risk the long winter journey.' On his return journey he stayed at Lyons, where he lodged in a gardener's cottage belonging to the Convent of the Visitation. Mother de Chaugy has given a wonderful account of a last meeting that occurred between Saint Francis and the co-founder of the Visitation: 'Mother', he said, 'we have some free hours together. Which of us shall start the conversation?' Mother de Chantal answered at once: 'May I, please, Father? My heart is in great need of being looked over by you.' 'What, Mother,' he answered, 'have you still keen desires and a wish to choose? I expected to find you entirely angelic.' And then he said: 'We shall talk about ourselves in Annecy. Now it is our duty to talk of the business of our congregation.'

Mother de Chantal immediately put away the notes she had made about the state of her soul and for four hours they discussed matters concerning the Visitation. As the end drew near, appalling remedies were applied to his body: 'A plaster of cantharides or blister-beetles was applied to his bald head, the effect of which is distressing especially to a patient in public view, for there appears to have been no privacy during this unhappy scene.' Then he was lifted out of bed and placed in a chair. The doctors asked him whether he would agree to being cauterised. 'My body is in the doctors' hands; let them do what they think best.' A priest reminded the patient to unite his sufferings with the crown of thorns. He murmured in protest that there could be no comparison. As the cruel, but well-intentioned treatment was carried still further, he murmured 'Jesus Maria' and that evening he died.

He was beatified on 28 December 1661, thirty-nine years to the day after his death, and canonised on 19 April 1665 – Good Shepherd Sunday.

Soon his *Introduction to the Devout Life* was being read all over France. Queen Maria de Medici sent a copy in a jewelled binding to James I who carried it around with him. It has proved to be one of the best-sellers of devotional literature, not only among Catholics, but among Christian people of all communions. *Every Man's Book of Saints* says 'It is for his holiness and his spiritual vision that all Catholics may gratefully commemorate Francis in these more ecumenical days.'

Most of us who read any spiritual books have the feeling that the *Introduction to the Devout Life* is unlike any other. It sets out to help the ordinary lay person towards spiritual perfection. The first English translation appeared in 1913. At the time it was revolutionary. *The Imitation of Christ* by Thomas à Kempis has proved an inspiration to laymen without number, from Mr Gladstone downwards. But on the face of it is another monkish book, written by a monk for monks. The nearest approach that I can find to the *Introduction to the Devout Life*, written three and a half centuries later, is Cardinal Hume's *Searching for God*. That book is based on addresses given by the Abbot of Ampleforth to his monks. Somehow, perhaps because he had been a housemaster and, for that matter, a rugby football coach to the great school attached, every word comes straight across to the layman.

The treatise on *The Love of God* is less obviously designed for the ordinary person, but the zealous layman, if he persists, can apply it to his own problems just as directly. In each case, the statement of St John, 'God is love', is the basis on which Francis's religious system is founded. The love of God, that is to say, God's love, has selected human nature to bind itself with in the person of the heavenly Son. Each individual man becomes the mirror of Christ. Even here below man is to be a partaker of the divine nature, and afterwards partakes of God's eternal glory in heaven.

For St Francis de Sales 'the great question was to show that the love of God was according to nature' (Müller, *St Francis de Sales*). Therefore he showed that the soul has a likeness to God and hence is capable of union with Him. He added that there is such an attraction to God in the natural predisposition of the soul that by virtue of his very essence man must long for God because God is truly 'the God of the human heart'.

'History,' again to quote Dr Müller, 'shows us two extreme trends of thought which both ended in heresy.' The under-estimation and even the complete disavowal of original sin and its results can be seen in ancient days with the Pelagians and modern times with Rousseau, and the philosophers of the French and Russian revolution. The logical consequence is an extreme version of the permissive society. If we are altogether good, there is no reason for placing any restraint on our complete freedom of action.

The opposite heresy, evident in the reformation and in Jansenism, insisted that the Fall meant complete corruption. The result was either an abandonment of any personal striving after moral perfection or the killing of all enjoyment in life and God. (A deadly pessimism, associated, not quite fairly perhaps, with Saint Augustine a thousand years earlier, was produced as an excuse or explanation.) Saint Francis de Sales takes the optimistic point of view, but made a distinction betwen a lower and a higher part of the soul. He wrote to a nun: 'You have two women in you; one is the daugher of Eve and hence of evil character.' The other 'has the will to obey God entirely, is the daugher of the Blessed Virgin Mary and therefore full of good endeavour'.

Francis identifies good with the personality itself and rejects evil as something essentially foreign to the higher man. Along with this goes his second fundamental belief: the doctrine of the redemption, and the emphasis on God's saving grace which comes to every man's aid.

The austere theologian Tertullian, for example, has described the relationship between God and man as similar to that of master and slave. Others have gone further and likened the relationship to that of master and dog. The normal relationship of the soul to God, according to Francis's teaching, is that of a child to its father, or like that between queen and king. In his own lifetime many theological writers were scandalised by this doctrine. They bewailed his 'lack of respect for God'. They felt that Saint Francis's attitude ruined the necessary foundation of humility and the trembling of the soul before God's majesty. Yet in the Lord's prayer we are told: 'Thus should ye pray: Our Father'. He is called Father, nor ruler or Lord or judge.

The contrast between Saint Francis and earlier spiritual writers emerges most clearly from his views on humility and confidence. Saint Augustine wrote: 'You should hate your own work in yourself and love God's work in you.' In his *Confessions* he proclaims to the world 'All sins and faults are my own. All that is valuable in me is the gift of God.'

Saint Thomas Aquinas took over Saint Augustine's doctrine and fused it with Aristotle. 'Man can be considered in two ways', said Saint Thomas 'according to what is of God and what is of man'. Of man is every imperfection, of God is every perfection and all the means of salvation. The author of *The Imitation of Christ* wrote even more starkly: 'Who am I, prays the writer, that I should dare to talk to thee, my Lord and God? I am thy poorest servant, a prostrate worm, much poorer and more wretched than I know. Remember, Oh Lord, that I am nothing, have nothing and can do nothing.' All this, while it may or may not be salutary, is very depressing. Saint Francis de Sales was not the first writer to recognise the dangers of such extreme pessimism.

Saint Teresa of Avila saw the danger of discouragement which is bound to come from this attitude. 'If we never get from this swamp of our misery,' she writes, 'we will suffer great damage. . . . A thousand thoughts upset the soul and lead it astray. . . . For example, dare I risk to undertake this or that? Is it not arrogance for such a miserable creature as I to be busied about something so

noble as interior prayer?' She adds this in regard to humility:
'Many people think it is humility not to recognise the gifts God has
bestowed on them. . . . Of course God bestows the gifts without
our meriting them. But we must be thankful to his majesty for
them. For if we do not recognise what we have recieved from him,
we will not awake to his love.' In other words, we must on no
account fail to love the person that we are, all the more because
that person has been created by God.

Francis, following Saint Teresa and other sixteenth century
Spanish mystics, waxed lyrical about the soul: 'O my little lovely
soul, thou that canst know and love God, why dost thou take
delight in trivial things? Thou hast an eternity to struggle for. Why
dost thou want to delight in a moment?' But that did not rule out,
indeed it paved the way, to an extreme joyfulness in this life below.
'God' he wrote 'is the God of joy. The spirit of joy is the true spirit
of devotion. Live joyfully,' he cried. 'Our Lord is looking down on
you lovingly.' In the spiritual philosophy of Saint Francis
humility, confidence and joy were inseparable.

This spiritual attitude led on to one of the most characteristic of
all his doctrines – his view of human perfection. 'God created man
after his image and likeness. The most perfect man is the man in
whom this likeness is implanted most deeply.' But perfection is not
a ready-made form into which each individual can be moulded to
become a ready-made saint. True love of God leads human desire
to conformity with the will of God. The perfect Christian affirms
his personality as it was created by God. Each of us must live our
life in certain circumstances and blessed or cursed by certain
human characteristics. 'Nothing,' Saint Francis wrote, 'hinders
our perfection so much as the longing for another condition.' Saint
Francis became the extreme exponent of the spiritual possibilities
of life in the world, while never losing sight of the unique
possibilities inherent in the religious vocation.

St Francis was not on the side of those who eliminated all
natural feelings, for example joy in possession and sorrow over
loss. The Gospels showed clearly that Jesus' love for individual
men and women was deep and warm. 'Francis' love of God is full
of warmth and it is this same love that extends over His whole
creation' (Müller). Francis loved his family and friends with the
greatest tenderness.

Pope Pius XI as we have seen, singled out St Francis de Sales as the spiritual writer best suited to meet the religious needs of the contemporary world. Certainly it is easier to set off in his spiritual direction than in that of any other of the great saints. Of all the saints he seems to put himself most obviously alongside ordinary men and women.

14
ST VINCENT DE PAUL
1581–1660

Anyone remotely concerned with the care of the poor and the distressed will place St Vincent de Paul near the top of their list of saints. For me, he will always be the saint of the outcasts. The picture of him, however, as the patron saint of social work is, according to the best judges, incomplete. The Abbé Bremond, for example, wrote: 'Whoever sees him as more of a philanthropist than a mystic, whoever does not see him as a mystic before everything else, forms a picture of a Vincent de Paul who never existed.' The Abbé does not hesitate to describe him as 'the greatest of our men of action'. But he returns again and again to what seemed to him the saint's more spiritual qualities.

St Vincent de Paul was widely recognised as a saint in his later years, but his career was by no means a smooth success story. He was a native of Pouy, a village in Gascony, where he was born in 1581. His parents occupied a very small farm, bringing up four sons and two daughters, Vincent being their third child. At the age of twelve, he was entrusted to the care of the Franciscans at Dax, who undertook to teach him for the sum of sixty francs a year which, somehow or other, his poor family managed to pay. The young man attracted the attention of a lawyer in the district, who committed to him the education of his children and assisted him towards the priesthood.

On 23 September 1600, Vincent was ordained a priest by Francois de Bourdeilles, Bishop of Périgueux, in the chapel of his palace at St Julien, now Château-l'Evêque. Vincent was then nineteen-and-a-half. Five years later, returning from Marseilles to Toulouse, he underwent an appalling experience. He himself described the episode with his usual good humour. He was travelling by sea when three 'Turkish brigantines gave chase and attacked us so vigorously that two or three of our men were killed and the rest wounded. I got hurt by an arrow, which will mark the date of the occurrence for me all my life; so there was nothing for it but to yield to the rascals, who were really worse than wild beasts.' After startling adventures, he eventually became the slave of an 'apostate', who assisted him to escape and himself was reconciled to the faith.

All through his life, St Vincent possessed an almost magical gift of winning the confidence of important persons, along with humbler souls. At Avignon he came to the notice of Cardinal Montorio, the Pope's Vice-Legate, whom he accompanied to Rome. Here he continued his theological studies until he was entrusted by three eminent persons with a secret mission to the King of France. No one seems clear as to the nature of this mission. It is at least certain that he was several times admitted to an audience with Henry IV. His prospects however were by no means encouraging when at the beginning of the year 1610 he was granted a small benefice becoming the chaplain to Queen Marguérite de Valois, Henry IV's first wife.

Vincent now, in the words of the biographer Emmanuel de Broglie 'had the opportunity of making close acquaintance with the great and powerful of this world, and of walking over ground covered with snares without tripping. The son of the peasant of the Landes had too much native shrewdness, too much natural tact, and his soul was likewise too full of the Christian simplicity which goes steadily through the greatest difficulties, to be perplexed or led astray by the brilliant *entourage* with which he was so closely connected.'

Father Leonard, CM, in his edition of the letters of St Vincent de Paul, pauses at this point to consider 'the young Gascon priest' as he appeared to his contemporaries in Paris in the year 1610: 'He was of medium height, well-built and well-proportioned. His hair was dark, his complexion brown and he wore the slight moustache and short closely-cropped beard then usual with the French clergy. He had a remarkable head, the brow was high, broad and "majestic", the nose large and fleshy, the jaw square and determined, the chin square and strong, the mouth wide and close-lipped. But by far the most striking feature of his countenance was the eyes. Anyone who has even glanced casually at the portrait in the sacristy of the Fathers of the Mission, Rue de Sèvres, Paris, cannot fail to be struck with, and perhaps even slightly disconcerted by, those dark, deep-set eyes twinkling with mischief, irony and humour . . . .'

In 1610, he was a good priest of ordinary virtue, of a strongly empirical cast of mind, energetic, decided, sensible, straight-foward and courageous, with a talent to comprehend a situation and to act promptly. He had a hatred of humbug and, above all, he was tenacious and ambitious. His available correspondence stops in 1610, not to begin again until 1625. It is accepted that between the years 1609 and 1611 he was 'converted', that is to say (in Father Leonard's phrase) 'set upon the road that leads to as perfect a human holiness as may be attained in this life'. He took the overwhelming decision to devote his life to the service of the poor, apparently in a deliberate determination to resist temptation against the faith.

He certainly owed much to Monsieur de Berulle, the future cardinal. At the latter's suggestion, he accepted the cure of Clichy in 1612, and in the following year became tutor to the sons of Emanuel de Gombi, General of the Galleys, and the spiritual guide of his wife. Except for a brief departure in 1617, to a remote parish, he remained with the Gombis until the year 1635. They gave him great help in fulfilling his vocation, and he gave them spiritual help.

Madame de Gombi assisted him in establishing a company of missionaries to serve their tenants and the people of the country-side in general. A new community was formed, whose members were to renounce the ecclesiastical preferments and to devote themselves to the smaller towns and villages. In 1625, the Countess died and Vincent went to live with his new congregation. In 1633, the prior of the canons regular of St Victor gave to this institute the priory of Saint-Lazare, which was made the chief house of the congregation, and thus the Fathers of the Mission are often called Lazarists, although sometimes Vincentians after their founder. They are a congregation of priests who make four simple vows of poverty, chastity, obedience and stability. They are employed in missions, especially among country people, and undertake the direction of diocesan and other seminaries. They now have colleges and missions in all parts of the world. St Vincent lived to see twenty-five houses founded in France, Piedmont, Poland and other places, including Madagascar.

For this initiative Pope Pius XII in 1957 picked out St Vincent de Paul, along with Mary Ward, as the real founders of lay action. The work undertaken under his inspiration by the laity in every parish was developed actively until the French Revolution. It was then suspended until re-established in 1833 in the form now known to us as the International Society of St Vincent de Paul

When the name of Vincent de Paul is uttered, the white cornetto of the Sisters of Charity rises before the mind's eye. They are regarded justly as the most fruitful and popular of all the works associated with St Vincent de Paul. They were originally established as confraternaties of charity to attend poor sick persons in each parish. They were distinguishable from nuns and lived in the world. Originally, St Vincent invoked the assistance of the wealthy women of Paris, banding them together as the Ladies of Charity to collect funds for, and assist in, his good work. Then he collected together 'a few country girls of lowly birth, but full of vigour and accustomed to work, and gave them to the ladies of the Confraternity of Charity as helpers, to replace them in the material work of which they were incapable, or which went too much against the grain' (Emmanuel de Broglie). Gradually it became a classless order which expanded beyond all expectations.

St Vincent did much work among the galley slaves confined in the Conciergerie. He was officially appointed chaplain to the Galleys (of which Philip de Gondi was General). In 1622, he gave a mission for the convicts in the galleys at Bordeaux. There is one story told of him in this connection which one would certainly like to feel was true. St Vincent, in the course of his visit to the convicts, was so touched by the fears and despair of a young man who was being torn from the arms of his wife, that he took the place of the galley-slave. He seated himself on the bench to take the oar, suffered his legs to be put in irons and began to row, full of divine joy at suffering such torment for the crucified Jesus. It is said that to the end of his life he bore the marks of the irons.

As the years passed, St Vincent de Paul became more and more of a national, even an international figure, and more and more involved in high affairs of state. In 1643 (?), soon after the death of Louis XIII, he was appointed by the Queen Regent Anne of Austria to the 'Council of Conscience'. He joined the Council with reluctance, hoping to confine his attention solely to ecclesiastical affairs and to business directly concerned with the spiritual and temporal welfare of the poor and afflicted. However, before long he became indispensable to the Council and, in Father Leonard's phrase, its chief agent for good.

But there were many and glaring abuses in the Church at that time, with which St Vincent wrestled with limited success. The dominant figure in the Council, as in France, was Cardinal Mazarin. St Vincent's idealistic ideas interfered with Mazarin's policy of purchasing supporters by means of Church funds, and he removed Vincent from the Council.

A word must be said about St Vincent and the Frond, though the complications of the story defy any adequate summary. The Frond has been described as a revolution that failed. It was in fact, in its first phase, an attempt by the Parlement of Paris and, in its second, by the Princes of the Royal House, to modify, if not (according to some) to revolutionise the fundamental nature of the French monarchy, and to reverse both the home and foreign policy which Cardinal Richelieu had inaugurated, and which he relied on Mazarin to bring to a successful conclusion. The poor, as is usual in revolutionary periods, underwent extremes of suffering.

St Vincent was in the complicated position throughout of hating all the sins committed and loving all the sinners. As the second Frond collapsed, he was desperately anxious to persuade the Cardinal to abandon all ideas of suppressive measures against his opponents. He wrote to him, begging him not to inflame public opinion by entering Paris with the King and his mother when they returned to the city in triumph. A few extracts give the flavour: 'I summon up courage to write to you, Eminence . . . . Some may tell Your Eminence that your own private interests demand that the King should not pardon his people, and return to Paris without you, but that public affairs must be further embroiled and the war carried on, so as to make it clear that it is not Your Eminence who is stirring up the tempest, but certain evil-minded persons who are unwilling to submit to their prince.' He continues tactfully: 'I reply, my Lord, that it does not matter very much whether Your Eminence returns before or after the King does so, provided you do return, and that, once the King is re-established in Paris, His Majesty can recall you at his pleasure, and of that I am assured.' His earnest plea is wrapped up in a good deal of verbiage. He finishes by stating: 'I shall live and die in the obedience due to Your Eminence, whom Our Lord has committed me in this special manner. I assure you, My Lord, that I am your most humble, faithful and obedient servant.'

St Vincent carried on with his social endeavours to the last. In the autumn of 1660 he died calmly in his chair, aged seventy-nine. He was canonised by Pope Clement XII in 1737. Pope Leo XIII proclaimed him patron of all charitable societies. Outstanding among them is the society that bears his name and is infused with his spirit, founded by Frederick Ozoman in Paris in 1835.

The Abbé Bremond insists that we must put aside any concept of 'the dear old saint, the crafty peasant, the commonplace, tottering mendicant prior that has been pictured for us'. On the contrary, St Vincent was 'many-sided, subtle, rich in fine shades, unusual and most attractive'. The Abbé regrets that St Vincent often referred to himself as a peasant, for this he feels has left the misleading impression. He considers that his gift for under-estimating himself and being amusing at his own expense has contributed to the same misconception. St Vincent has been criticised for an excessive degree of humility, a complaint not infrequently levelled against a saint. In St Vincent's case at least there was nothing remotely artificial. 'Is there', he once asked, 'a single man on this earth who has such a high opinion of his virtue to believe he is in a state to receive Holy Communion worthily?'

If we wish for St Vincent's monument, we have only got to look around us and to admire the spirit of charity which he so widely disseminated. But he would wish the last word to be of a different character. 'The inner life,' he said, 'is necessary. We must strive for it. If anyone is wanting in it, he is wanting in everything.' What he achieved in this world sprang from his unending communion with a better world than this.

15
ST TERESA OF LISIEUX
1873–1897

At the end of the 1950s, Father Vernon Johnson wrote the Introduction to Monsignor Ronald Knox's new translation of the autobiography of St Teresa of Lisieux. 'No modern saint,' he submitted with confidence, 'has exerted such an influence on the men and women of our time as St Teresa of Lisieux.' There appears to be a trend towards saints who have done great things in the world; towards men and women of action rather than of contemplation or, as in the case of St Teresa of Avila and St Ignatius, of action combined with contemplation. Moreover, the twentieth century has had all too full a share of martyrs. Nevertheless the informed interest in Teresa of Lisieux's spirituality is as keen as ever. New studies of her appear at regular intervals. It still seems that 'no modern saint has exerted such an influence' as she has. Too late have I loved her, to adapt the words of St Augustine. But now every time I read something new relating to her I become more entranced.

The external facts of her life are unremarkable. Her parents were Louis-Martin, a watchmaker of Alençon, son of an officer in the armies of Napoleon I, and Azelie-Marie Guerin, a maker of *point d'Alençon* lace in the same town. There were nine children, of whom five survived to maturity. All became nuns, including the youngest, the future St Teresa.

She was born on 2 January 1873. In 1877 Mme Martin died; M Martin sold his business at Alençon and went to live at Lisieux. Teresa was specially cared for by her elder sister Pauline. When Teresa was nine, Pauline entered the Carmel convent at Lisieux; Teresa began to be drawn in the same direction. When she was fourteen, she underwent an experience which ever afterwards she referred to as her 'conversion'. In retrospect it is clear that from the earliest days she was not only brought up in a deeply religious atmosphere, but was full of love for Jesus and complete certainty about the prime truths of religion.

One of her mother's letters contained this passage (her mother, as already mentioned, died when Teresa was four years old): 'Baby is such a queer little creature as you never saw; she comes up and puts her arms around me and wishes I were dead. "Oh, poor little Mother," she says, "I do wish you'd die." Then when you scold her, she explains: "Oh, but it's only because I want you to go to Heaven; you told me yourself one can't go to Heaven without dying." She wants to kill off her father too, when she gets really affectionate.'

When Teresa was fourteen, she became very anxious to enter Carmel like two of her sisters, but both the Carmelite authorities and the Bishop of Bayeux refused to hear of it on account of her age. A few months later she was in Rome with her father and a French pilgrimage on the occasion of the jubilee of Pope Leo XIII. When her turn came to kneel for the Pope's blessing, she boldly broke the rule of silence.

> 'Most Holy Father,' I said, 'I've a great favour to ask of you.' He bent towards me till his head was nearly touching my face, and his dark, deep-set eyes seemed to look right down into the depths of my soul. 'Most Holy Father,' I said, 'in honour of your jubilee, I want you to let me enter the Carmelite Order at fifteen.' The Holy Father looked at me with great kindness, but all he said was: 'Very well my child, do what your superiors tell you.' I put both my hands on his knees and had one more try: 'Yes, but if you'd say the word, Most Holy Father, everybody would agree.' He fixed his eyes on me and said, emphasising every syllable as he uttered it: 'All's well, all's well; if God wants you to enter, you will.' He spoke with such earnestness and such conviction that I can still hear him saying it.

At the end of the year the bishop gave permission. On 9 April 1888, aged fifteen, she entered the Carmel convent, where she remained till her death nine years later.

In 1889 her father's mind gave way after two paralytic attacks. He had to be removed to a private asylum, where he remained for three years. Even St Teresa's most sympathetic admirers must have some difficulty with her comment: 'The three years of my father's martyrdom seem to me the dearest and most fruitful of my life. I would not exchange them for the most sublime ecstasies.' That may be true of her own suffering, but what about the suffering of her father?

In 1893 she became Novice Mistress in all but name, and between January 1895 and January 1896 she wrote the bulk of what became her immortal autobiography, at the request of the Reverend Mother Agnes, then Prioress, her sister Pauline. It was supplemented by two other documents: a letter to Sister Marie of the Sacred Heart (her eldest sister Marie), written at her request in three days between 13 and 16 September 1896, and a notebook written for the Reverend Mother Marie de Gonzague, begun on 3 June and finished early in July 1897.

On Good Friday 1896, that is after the first part of her autobiography was completed, she underwent an extraordinary experience. Most people would call it tragic, certainly in one so young, but she saw it quite differently:

> I had never felt so strong, and this strengh lasted me till Easter. But on Good Friday Jesus had a present for me – nothing less than the hope of seeing him quite soon, in heaven. What a wonderful day to look back on! I went up to bed, after watching till midnight at the altar of repose, and I had scarcely laid my head on the pillow when I became conscious of what seemed like a warm tide that rose up till it reached my lips. I wasn't sure what it was, but my soul was flooded with joy at the thought that I was going to die; surely I must be spitting blood . . . .

And so it proved she was. Her disease moved remorselessly forward. In June 1897 she was transferred to the infirmary of the convent, never to leave it again. She died on 30 September 1897. On her lips, to quote Butler's *Lives of the Saints*: 'were words of divine love'.

The autobiography, *The Story of a Soul*, was first published on 30 September 1898, in a version heavily edited by Mother Agnes. The original text was not published for another half century. Two thousand copies were printed. The book, first read in the convent, was then lent to chosen friends. Soon the Carmel of Lisieux was inundated with orders for copies from all parts of France. Numbers of young women desired to enter the convent of Lisieux. They came first of all from France and then from Ireland, Italy, Portugal, Turkey and even the Argentine.

Teresa was beatified by Pope Pius XI in 1923 and the same Pope in 1925 declared her to have been a saint. No doubt it was the enormous popularity of the autobiography that led ultimately to these sublime honours. But it was not the only factor. Seven volumes entitled *A Rain of Roses* were produced by the Carmel of Lisieux. Teresa's promise that she would send down this 'shower' when once she had reached heaven was being amply fulfilled.

Two examples of her miracles can be given here. There was a Bishop of the Upper Congo who persuaded her to cure a missionary attacked by sleeping sickness and who, although he had asked no favour for himself, was incidentally cured of his own chronic and disabling rheumatism. And a prioress of a Carmel in southern Italy, having an urgent debt to pay off, found the needed banknotes miraculously placed in an empty drawer of her writing table. The list of miracles goes on and on, involving not just devout Catholics, but a Presbyterian minister, a sceptical journalist and many others.

What was there so extraordinary about the personality and, inextricably linked with it, the message of this young woman? I can speak for many others when I say that I came to the story of her life with no predisposition in her favour. There seemed to be something sentimental and gushing which put me off. But once I was well into the autobiography I was won over, like such a vast multitude of others.

The simple programme of the 'little way' sprang from an equally simple source – an all-consuming love of Jesus Christ, which is usually taken to sum up her doctrine. Mother Agnes once asked her: 'What is the little way that you would teach?' Teresa answered: 'It is the way of spiritual childhood, the way of trust and absolute self-surrender. I want to point out to souls the means I have always found so completely successful, to tell them there is only one thing to do here below – to offer our Lord the flowers of *little sacrifices* and win Him by our caresses. This is how I have won Him, and that is why I shall be made welcome.'

Teresa had always longed to be a saint, 'but,' she said, 'I have always felt that I am so far removed from them as a grain of sand trampled underfoot by a passer-by is from the mountain whose summit is lost in the clouds.' She was convinced that it was impossible for her to become great. 'But I will seek out a means of reaching Heaven by a little way – very short, very straight and entirely new. We live in an age of inventions: there are now lifts which save us the trouble of climbing stairs. I will try and find a lift by which I may be raised to God, for I am too small to climb the steep stairway of perfection.' At this point she speaks for all of us, with our yearning for perfection and our over-whelming consciousness of frailty. The 'little way' seems, at least until we have tried it, to be open to everyone.

'It remained for her,' writes Vita Sackville-West, 'to work out her plan in detail, to find a comprehensive formula for her famous "little way". Never to fail in the smallest particular; never the slightest relaxation of vigilance; the minutest slip on the self-imposed path to be instantly corrected and the balance restored; to act not dutifully but joyfully; to train the character by incessant practice until the eclipsing of the self became second nature.'

In her autobiography, Teresa gives a number of examples of small acts of charity which involved some sacrifice or at any rate deliberate self-control on her part. She did not find it easy to like everyone. 'For example,' she writes: 'I ought to single out sisters who are the least attractive to me, roadside casualties who need a good samaritan. It is a little surprising to find a number of these in a convent where all have dedicated their lives to God.'

Many know the story of the nun (and she was not the only one) who irritated St Teresa exceedingly. St Teresa set out to show her such goodwill that the nun finally asked her: 'What is there about me that you find so attractive?' Incidentally, an indiscretion by a priest attached to the convent revealed many years later to the sister in question that she was the highly unattractive figure described.

One other example gives the flavour of many of the anecdotes.

I was helping to do the washing, and there was a sister opposite me who managed to splash my face with dirty water every time she lifted up the handkerchiefs from the ledge. My first instinct was to step back and wipe my face, by way of suggesting to this over-effusive sister that I should be obliged if she would keep herself to herself. But all at once the thought occurred to me: 'You're a fool not to take what's going free.' So I took care to hide my annoyance. I devoted myself instead to cultivating a taste for dirty water, and really in the end I was so fond of this new kind of sprinkling that I determined to come back another time to this lucky dip where one was so well treated!

So much is straightforward, on the surface at least. Here is a way of life which all of us could at least attempt to lead. But when we come to the question of her approach to suffering, it is harder to go along with her doctrine. 'From her early days,' points out Father

Michael Hollings in his penetrating study of Teresa of Lisieux, 'Teresa had an intense desire for sacrifice, mortification and even martyrdom.' Later on, when she wrote in her autobiography: 'I realise that to become a saint one must suffer much', she recalled that even in the days of her childhood she had cried out: 'My God, I choose everything – I will not be a saint by halves. I am not afraid of suffering for Thee. One thing only do I fear, and that is to follow my own will. Accept then the offering I make of it. I choose *all* that Thou willest.'

At the end of her life, someone, presumably another nun, was foolish enough to say: 'They say that you have never suffered much . . .'. Teresa replied: 'I have drunk the most delicious wine but to me it has been full of bitterness. I say bitterness, yet after all my life has not been sad, because I have learned to find joy and sweetness in all that is bitter.' 'You are suffering just now, are you not?' 'Yes,' she answered, 'but I have longed so much to suffer.'

For most of us, there is something incomprehensible here. Teresa endured great physical suffering in her last eighteen months. But to quote Father Hollings again: 'The greatest trial was not one which came from within Carmel. It was one for Teresa herself and for her relationship with the Lord. One night she said to Mother Agnes: "Last night I was seized with a terrible feeling of anguish. I was lost in darkness from out of which came an accursed voice: Are you sure God loves you? Has He come to tell you so Himself? The opinon of a few creatures will not justify you in His sight." ' Right up to the end of her life she was oppressed by spiritual anxieties. She welcomed or even rejoiced in them.

Speaking more generally, ought we to be subscribing to her doctrine of suffering as it applied in her own case or, more urgently, in ours? Daniel Morris, a leading Catholic journalist in America, has written a notable little book called *Beatitude Saints*, comparing a number of canonised men and women with spiritual leaders of our time. He matches Teresa of Lisieux with Dorothy Day, the lifelong champion of the poor in America, who wrote a biography of Teresa, on the face of it a figure utterly unlike herself. 'I shook my head,' he writes, 'over and over again as I read Dorothy's accounts of Teresa's various forms of suffering. At times there seemed to be an almost unhealthy penchant for pain. I can understand how penance as an atonement for sin serves to cleanse the soul and psyche. But I can describe only as mysterious or mystical both Dorothy's and Teresa's literal need for suffering.'

Daniel Morris does not feel that he has come up with any totally satisfying answers. He certainly does not reach the conclusion that this 'obsession with detachment, suffering and near-personal abuse must be the road to holiness'. He recognises that it was a way chosen by Teresa with heroic results. 'My mortification,' she wrote, 'consists in checking my self-will, keeping back an impatient word, doing little things for those around me without their knowing it and countless things like that.'

But that might be described as an extreme form of unselfishness. What extra value is achieved by suffering from outside? No doubt the first answer must be that suffering provides a unique opportunity for accepting the will of God and the sheer acceptance is itself of spiritual benefit to oneself. But how are others benefited? Here Teresa's words must be quoted: 'Suffering opened her arms to me, and I threw myself into them lovingly enough . . . . Our Lord let me see clearly that if I wanted to win souls, I had got to do it by bearing a cross. So the more suffering came my way, the more strongly did suffering attract me.'

Here we are confronted with the fundamental doctrine of redemptive suffering. The death of Christ on the cross to save mankind is of course the supreme example. It is impossible to work out Saint Teresa's message in academic propositions, though she had for an untrained girl an excellent analytical intellect. It is impossible to distinguish her love of suffering from her love of Christ. Each of the three parts of her autobiography ends on the same note: 'Love can only be repaid by love . . . . Dear Jesus, I implore you to look down in mercy on a whole multitude of souls that share my littleness, to choose out for yourself a whole legion of victims, so little as to be worthy of your love . . . . I know what tenderness God has for any prodigal child of his that comes back to Him . . . . It is not just because God in his undeserved mercy has kept my soul clear of mortal sin that I fly to Him on the wings of confidence and love.'

16

ST MAXIMILIAN KOLBE
1894–1941

Maximilian Kolbe is the only one of our selected canonised saints who lived during the twentieth century. The heroic action which had brought Kolbe immortal fame took place either the last day of July or the first of August 1941. The Auschwitz sirens announced the escape of a prisoner. It was known that for every prisoner who escaped, ten of his fellows must die. 'And this was the most terrible and the most feared way of death: a long, slow starvation, buried alive in especially constructed airless concrete underground bunkers' (*Candles in the Dark*, Mary Craig).

Early next morning the camp's Deputy Commandant, Karl Fritsch, accompanied by Gestapo chief Gerhardt Palitsch, slowly passed down the lines of the wretched prisoners, the officers' elegant uniforms contrasting painfully with the scarecrow rags of the men. Seven men were selected, then eight. When Fritsch pointed to the next man, tears trickled down the prisoner's hollow cheeks. 'Oh, please, please . . . my wife . . . my poor children. . . . Please spare me. I'm not old . . . I'm young. I can work, work hard for you . . . I don't want to die.' There was a commotion in the ranks and a rather small man, wearing spectacles in wire rims, stepped forward without permission. He walked briskly towards the group of SS men and stood to attention before Fritsch. What followed has been vividly described by Damien Walne and Joam Flory in *Totally Hers*:

'What is it? Who is it? Prisoners whispered amid the confusion. It's Father Kolbe. What, the Franciscan? Halt! gasped Fritsch. What do you want?'

As the guards moved in, the prisoner pointed to the man destined for death. 'Herr Commandant: I would like to take the place of this man . . . I would like to die in his place.'

The astounded Commandant turned to Palitsch and demanded: 'Who is this man? What is it all about?' Before the

German could answer, Maximilian Kolbe said quietly: 'I am a Catholic priest and I want to take his place. He has a wife, a family.' Kolbe's German was fluent. 'Are you crazy? An idiot?' snapped Fritsch. One of the SS men made to strike the priest with his cane, but Palitsch restrained him.

'I would like to die in his place,' the priest repeated. 'I'm of no use to anyone any more. This man is young and strong; he has a wife and family . . . I have no one . . .'.

Fritsch continued to stare at prisoner 16670 in amazement. Finally his eyes fell before the tranquil, deep brown ones of Maximilian Kolbe. He turned to Palitsch, anxious to end his embarrassment and said: 'Accepted'.

Francis Gajowniczek rejoined the ranks. Father Kolbe, prisoner 16670, was pushed in with the other prisoners already condemned to death.

At the canonisation ceremony on 17 October 1971, the present Pope, at that time Cardinal Karol Wojtyla, maintained that it was as a priest that Father Kolbe wished to die. His motive in giving his life was not merely to save a man but to help the other nine condemned men to die as Christians. In 1979, the Pope himself visited Auschwitz and saw, deeply moved, the cell in which Father Kolbe was ultimately killed by an injection of phenol.

On 10 October 1982, St Peter's Square in Rome was packed by 150,000 people for the solemn canonisation Mass of Father Kolbe. The heroism of Father Kolbe's death was the theme of the Pope's homily. He delivered it clothed in the red vestments of a martyr. 'Father Kolbe,' he said, 'himself a prisoner of Auschwitz, defended in that place of death the right to life of the innocent man, one of four millions. This man, Francis Gajowniczek, is still living and is here among us. Father Kolbe defended his right to life, declaring that he was ready to die in his place, because he was the father of a family and his life was necessary to his dear ones . . .'.

The Pope continued: 'Father Maximilian Mary Kolbe thus reaffirmed the Creator's exclusive right to the life of an innocent man and bore witness to Christ and love . . . and in this human death of his there was clear witness to Christ; witness born in Christ to the dignity of man; to the sanctity of his life and to the saving power of death in which the power of love is made manifest. . . . This was victory won over all the system of contempt and hate in man and what was divine in man, victory like that won by our Lord Jesus Christ on Calvary . . .'. The Pope concluded, 'And so, in virtue of my apostolic authority, I have decreed that Maximilian Mary Kolbe who, after beatification, was venerated as a confessor, shall henceforward be venerated as a martyr.'

Many deeds of heroism, sung and unsung, have been performed by men and women from whom nothing exceptional was expected; Father Kolbe's supreme act seemed to all who knew him to be entirely in character. Maximilian Kolbe was born on 8 January 1894 in Zdunska Wola, a village outside Lodz in that part of Poland which was ruled by Czarist Russia. He was given the name Ramund. His father was a poor weaver and ardent patriot. He and his wife were both Catholics with a strong devotion to the Blessed Virgin. There is a well-attested story that, on one occasion, Ramund, a rather naughty small boy, exasperated his mother so that she wondered aloud what would become of him. Seven-year-old Ramund, stricken by her distress rushed, in tears, to the church where he put the same question about his future to the Virgin Mary. Mary appeared to him, holding two crowns, offering him a choice between a white and a red one. The white one signified life-long purity, the red promised a martyr's crown. Ramund told Mary in the vision that he would take both.

The family were poor, but Ramund showed brilliant promise. The time came when he asked to be admitted as a novice Franciscan. He was given a new name after a third-century Roman citizen from Carthage who had been executed for refusing to serve in the Roman Legion. 'I am a Christian,' he had declared, 'I cannot serve'.

Maximilian Kolbe, after taking temporary vows, was sent to Krakov to study philosophy, and thence to Rome. One of the professors called him a 'rare natural genius'. ('Fascinated by the exciting new idea of space travel, the young man produced a paper on the possibilities of inter-planetary and inter-stellar travel, backed by calculations and detailed drawings' (Mary Craig).)

But Kolbe wanted only one thing – to become a priest. At this time 'the first signs of tuberculosis began to appear; the poor circulation, haemorrhages, headaches and intolerable tension that would plague him for the rest of his days'. The extraordinary range of Father Kolbe's spiritual ambitions, not for himself, but for the world, and for what he could accomplish in the rescue of souls was revealed on 17 October 1918 in Rome when he was twenty-three.

He and six confrères – he was always the moving spirit –
founded the Militia Immaculatae. The friars had for a long time
toyed with the idea of founding an organisation to combat evil in
the world and to conquer the hearts of men, then pitted against
each other in mortal global confrontation. Furthermore the war,
in 1917, was at its most destructive with the invention of new
weapons of death, and there was no end in sight. Father Kolbe was
fully convinced that there was only one person capable of bringing
the world back to God, and that was Mary Immaculate.

Did any saint, even St Ignatius of Loyola, ever entertain so far-
reaching or audacious a spiritual project? The act of consecration
read and signed on the night of the founding of the Militia
Immaculatae shows the amazing degree of Maximilian Kolbe's
commitment to Our Lady and his complete confidence in her
ability to work through him and indeed through all those who
dedicate their lives to her:

> Mary Immaculate is our ideal. Through her, we wish to gain for Christ
> all souls in the whole world, both those who are living and those yet to
> be born. To come nearer to her, to become like her, to allow her to reign
> in our hearts and the whole of our being, that she may live and work in
> us and through us, that she may love God with our heart, that we may
> belong to her unreservedly . . . this is our ideal. To diffuse light over
> our surroundings, to win souls for her and that she may reign in the
> hearts of all in whatever part of the world they may be, without
> discrimination as to race, nationality, language, even in the hearts of
> the still unborn until the end of time. This is our ideal.

Maximilian Kolbe was ordained a priest in April 1918. (Poland
was liberated and became, after a century and a half of subjection,
a free country at the end of the year.) Early in 1919, Maximilian
returned to Poland to teach philosophy and Church history in the
Franciscan seminary in Krakov. In the next twenty years, he
achieved phenomenal success in his Christian crusade, in his
establishment of religious communities and in his publication of
newspapers with mass circulation. By the outbreak of the Second
World War scarcely a Catholic home in Poland was without one of
his publications.

He founded a friary which eventually contained 762 friars, the
largest number of any friary in the world. It was called Niepokalanov, 'Place of the Immaculate One', and was built by the

friars with their bare hands throughout a freezing winter. They published a very successful magazine, *The Knight of the Immaculate*. The machinery for their printing presses was the finest that modern technology could provide, but the friars themselves lived in true Franciscan poverty.

Kolbe spent the years 1930–36 in Japan. The mission came about in this way. One day on a train Maximilian met a group of young Japanese students who 'charmed him by their kindness and courtesy' (Mary Craig). Acting on impulse, he asked his superiors to send him to Japan to establish a friary there. To his amazement they agreed. Before he set off for Japan, someone asked him what he was going to do for money. 'Money?' he echoed in surprise, 'Oh, it will turn up somehow. Mary will see to that. It's her business and her Son's.'

Kolbe and his colleagues had no knowledge of Japanese, but nothing deterred them. A friary was established, a printing works and seminary. By 1936, he was able to report much progress in Japan. He had plans to extend the work to India, but his superiors saw the state of his health and brought him back to Niepokalanov.

At the time of Father Kolbe's canonisation, some accusations of anti-Semitism were levelled against him. In his absence a national daily paper produced at Niepokalanov was guilty of anti-Semitic sentiments, but Father Kolbe was thousands of miles away at that time. From 1939 onwards, he laboured without stint to aid and succour the Jews as their persecution mounted in ferocity.

The war broke out on 1 September 1939; Father Kolbe and the remaining friars were immediately harassed. Father Kolbe devoted himself to the refugees seeking asylum in Niepokalanov. About 3,000 refugees and deportees passed through his hands, among them about 2,000 Jews. The friars shared everything they had with these unhappy men, women and children. 'We must do everything in our power to help these unfortunate people driven from their homes and deprived of even the most basic necessities,' said Father Maximilian. 'Our mission in the coming months is among them.'

He persuaded the German authorities, with much difficulty, to grant permission to continue with the publication of his paper *Knight*, of which 120,000 copies were printed. In the last editorial he was ever to write, Maximilian expressed a profound conviction:

No one in the world can change Truth. What we can and should do is to seek Truth and serve it when we have found it. The real conflict is within. Beyond armies of occupation and the hecatombs of the extermination camps, two irreconcilable enemies lie in the depths of every soul. And of what use are the victories on the battlefield, if we are defeated in our innermost personal selves?

But he was under no illusion that he would be allowed to continue for long in freedom. The Gestapo came for him on 17 February 1941. The previous evening he had asked if he could share supper with some of the older friars. Next morning, he had risen early and made the rounds of all the brothers who were sick. It was his way of saying goodbye.

He was taken first to Pawaik, a horrible prison in the centre of Warsaw. 'One of the SS guards, infuriated at the sight of a Franciscan priest handed over to him, tore at the rosary which girdled the priest's waist, thrusting the crucifix in his face. "Do you believe in that?" he shouted contemptuously. When the Franciscan replied: "I do", the guard struck him a vicious blow in the face. He repeated the question and, receiving the same reply, began to rain blows upon the priest's head and shoulders. A fellow prisoner, Edward Gniadek, later witnessed to Father Maximilian's calm self-control. "Don't be upset for me," the priest whispered to this man, when the SS guard had finally made off. "You have enough to worry about and, in any case, it is all for Mary Immaculate." "He behaved," said Gniadek wonderingly, "as though nothing untoward had happened."'

On 28 May, with more than three hundred other prisoners, Father Kolbe was herded into a cattle truck without food or water, and sent to Auschwitz concentration camp. As the trucks moved off on their long journey, his voice could be heard leading the others in a hymn to Mary Immaculate.

It is impossible to recount here the numerous stories of Christian heroism and the appalling maltreatment in Auschwitz. Many recollections of this kind are provided during the canonisation process. What seems to have made an even deeper impression than his personal stoicism was his almost supernatural power to provide support and consolation to his fellow victims. Monsignor Szweda's testimony must serve in place of many others. 'Don't you see it,' said Father Kolbe, 'as an honour to suffer? Just think Jesus has chosen us to share his sufferings. Don't forget He too was persecuted and rejected by all. He knew indescribable sadness and exhaustion. They beat Him, nailed Him to the Cross, ridiculed Him, just as they ridicule us. But He forgave them, and so should we.'

Father Kolbe was serene in the conviction that he himself would meet his death in the camp. But he sustained Monsignor Szweda in all his darkest moments. 'You,' he said, 'will survive the camp and you will give witness to the truth, but on one condition only – that you trust in Mary. Do not count on your own strength, nor on that of other people, but on Mary and God. Grasp Mary with one hand and Jesus with the other, and then close your eyes and feel as safe as a child in the arms of its parents.' At all times he strove with every fibre of his being to help his comrades to win the ultimate victory of Auschwitz, to love and forgive their gaolers. No matter how bruised and battered he was, and no matter what the risk, he still heard confessions, preached and said Mass, all of which activities were punishable by death.

Bruno Bergewiecz, a Pole, was the secretary and interpreter of the punishment block. He was a frequent visitor to the death cell and was able to describe the death of Father Kolbe:

> Father Kolbe bravely held out. He asked for nothing. He did not complain. He inspired hope and confidence in others, repeating that the escapee might still be found and then they would be freed. At every inspection, Father Kolbe could be seen standing or kneeling in the middle, with a serene countenance looking at the arrivals. The SS men said among themselves: 'Such a priest as this we have never had here yet. He must be an extraordinary man.' Father Kolbe's gaze was indescribably penetrating . . . the SS men could not stand it and shouted: 'Look at the floor . . . don't look at us!'

After two weeks, only four were left, Father Kolbe among them. The cell was needed for other victims. The director of the infirmary, a German criminal, was instructed to administer an injection in the left arms of those still alive. 'With a prayer on his lips, Father Kolbe extended his arm to the executioner. As soon as the man left, I found Father Kolbe in a sitting position, leaning against the wall, his eyes open, his head bowed, his serenely beautiful face radiant.'

Franciszek Gajowniczek the man whose life was saved by Father Kolbe described it many years afterwards:

Father Kolbe was standing four or five men away from me. I cried out something about my poor wife and children and he stepped out of line and asked Lagerführer Fritzsch if he could take my place. He even tried to kiss the German's hand. It was the greatest miracle, for he could have been trampled underfoot or shot on the spot . . . . It is difficult for me to express my feelings at that moment. I had been sentenced to death and someone had offered his life for mine of his own free will. Was I dreaming? Was it true?

For a long time Gajowniczek felt conscience-stricken, but later he became convinced that he had been singled out to give witness to this heroic deed. He must become a missioner, he must survive to tell the world. He visited most countries of the world to talk about Father Kolbe's saintliness. What consoled him and gave him happiness was the thought that Father Kolbe's death was not in vain and that he was venerated as a saint of our time.

Pope John Paul II has frequently indicated a profound sense of identification with his fellow Pole, Father Kolbe. John Paul was twenty-one when the martydom occurred. From then on he was much influenced by the life and death of this humble friar; he has never ceased to proclaim his merits to the world.

It is appropriate that the twentieth century martyr in our selected list of saints should come from martyred Poland.

17

ST SERGIUS
1314–1392

ST SERAPHIM
1759–1832

Saint Sergius

Saint Sergius is, by common consent, the most popular and beloved of the saints of Russia. Saint Seraphim would be the supreme choice of a number of admirers, but Saint Sergius is beyond serious dispute the patron saint of Russia.

More than 300 years earlier, towards the end of the tenth century, the future Saint Vladimir had founded a great Christian state, which stretched from the Black Sea to the Baltic. The throne was usurped after his death by his adopted son. The two young princes, the rightful heirs, instead of resisting, disbanded their army and prepared for death. Prince Boris stood before the icon of the Saviour and prayed: 'Do not hold my brother responsible for this assassination as a sin'. Then he received communion and lay down peacefully. The assassins ran him through with their spears. His brother followed his example and was also murdered. The two princes were proclaimed as saints five years after their death on the insistence of the Russian people. Nevertheless the tradition of innocent suffering featured strongly thereafter in Russian spirituality.

In due course, a strong monastic tradition was established. But by the beginning of the fourteenth century, under the impact of the Tartar invasion there had been a sad retrogression. At the time of the birth of Sergius there was some monastic revival. But those responsible were hermits who had taken refuge in the virgin forests of Northern Russia where they lived a life of prayer and contemplation. Sergius, to start with, was a backward child. We are told that not only did he learn slowly but he was also unable to apply himself to his work. He was not as clever as his classmates. He was much scolded by his parents. He was frequently reprimanded by his teachers and fellow students.

He prayed ceaselessly that God would enable him to read and understand books. Then what can only be called a miracle occurred. He saw an old man praying under an oak. Bartholomew as he was then called told him about his life and his problems. The monk listened to him, prayed and gave him a little piece of prosphora which he had in his bag saying, 'Take and eat: this is given to you as a sign of the divine grace for reading. From this day on you will exceed your brothers and friends in your studies.' And so it proved. From that time Bartholomew began to read the Bible, liturgical books and the Church Fathers. 'Nevertheless,' to quote his biographer Pierre Kovalevsky, 'throughout his life he remained a man for whom the Christian experience was more important than learning or reason. He never wrote anything, and he drew his knowledge not from reading but from his continued communion with God. His vocation was not to speculative theology but rather to the application of the Gospel's precepts to life.'

In the event this has meant that he has left behind him no written doctrine. Yet it is not difficult, reading his life, to appreciate in some measure the reasons for his enormous influence. When his parents died he set off for the desert. He sold all his possessions and left his share of his father's will to his younger brother Peter. Leaving the world he and his brother Stephen went north into the forest of Radonezh. He was only twenty and not yet a monk. They visted the Metropolitan and received his blessing. He authorised them to build a chapel where they could sing the Office and pray waiting 'till a priest would celebrate the Liturgy there.' In the third year of his life 'he called on his desert abbot Metrophanes and asked him, with humility, bowing deeply before him, "My father, show charity to me and let me enter the monastic state. I have desired it since my youth, but the pleas of my parents held me back. Now, my lord and father, I am free and I thirst for living water (Ps.42)." The abbot immediately entered the church and received him as a monk.'

Before the old monk left Sergius said to him with great humility, 'Bless me, a humble monk and pray for my solitary life. Instruct me in how I should live alone in the desert and how I should pray to the Lord and how to resist the Enemy and his proud thoughts, for I am inexperienced and have just become a monk.'

When he first allowed 'certain God-fearing monks to join him in the wilderness', the saint inquired of them: 'Will you be able to suffer the hardships of this place, hunger and thirst and all kinds of privations?' They answered: 'Yes, venerable father, we want to suffer them, with the help of God and your prayers.' Saint Sergius, seeing their faith and zeal, wondered greatly, and said to them: 'Lords and brothers, I wanted to live alone in the desert until I should die in this place. But if it is God's will that there should be a monastery here, and that a great number of brethren should gather together, let God's will be done. I shall receive you gladly but you will have to build cells for yourselves. Now be it known to you: if you come to live in the desert, the beginning of all virtue is the fear of God.'

His asceticism emphasised labour, self-deprivation and patience rather than painful corporal punishment. There is the coarse and patched clothing, the lack of exterior authority, and the self-humiliation in the presence of subordinates and persons of humble condition. Many examples of his arresting humility are recorded. After spending three days without eating he approached one of the monks and said that he understood that the monk required a room in front of his cell. He himself would build it for him but would hope in return to be given a bowl of mouldy bread. He did not wish to receive this until he had finished the work. When all the work was done the old monk brought him the bowl, St Sergius ate this mouldy bread with water there being neither soup nor salt in the monastery.

His meekness was exhibited in a somewhat different way when his elder brother Stephen made himself objectionable. Sergius who had accepted the position of abbot with extreme reluctance left the monastery rather than assert his authority, preferring to offer an example of humility. He did not return for four years (1358–1362). Many miracles at various times were attributed to Sergius who had by now become a priest. Only one can be recounted here. The monks had begun to complain that Sergius had built his hermitage too far from an adequate water supply. He said to them 'I wanted to live alone but God wanted to establish a monastery to the glory of His name.' He immediately left the monastery, accompanied by one monk, went down into a little

ravine where there was a little water left from the rain, knelt down
and prayed. Then he blessed the spot and suddenly a plentiful
spring shot up, which supplies water for the monastery up to the
present day. Many pilgrims were cured by this water, and people
took it to the sick to heal them. They called it Sergius' fountain,
but the saint forbade this, saying that God, and not he, had given
this water to His unworthy servants.

Sergius might or might not have been remembered if he had
followed his own wishes and remained in his original monastery
though this became the famous monastery of the Holy Trinity.
Under a strong spiritual inspiration he became the founder of
many other monasteries directly and indirectly. The whole
monastic tradition of Russia must be derived from him more than
any other monk though, as already mentioned, such a tradition
had existed before his time. An authority on Russian spirituality,
G. P. Fedotov, expresses reservation about his external achievement. 'In the days of Saint Sergius,' he writes, 'that close union of
Church and State in Russia which is one of the chief characteristics of Russia's subsequent life as a nation had its origin. Saint
Sergius,' he goes on, 'yielding to new historical forces sees only the
blessings attendant upon a strong union of Church and State, not
the potentiality of evil likewise inherent in such a government.'
That may or may not be a fair historical verdict, but few will be
disposed to question the value of his spiritual message. He is
described correctly as the first Russian saint in whom mysticism is
observed but at no time did it weaken his sense of responsibility for
service to the world. He comforted, healed and protected the
oppressed. From that day to this, even since the Communist
revolution, the Trinity-Saint Sergius Monastery has been the
centre of theological studies in Russia.

Many attempts have been made with limited success to sum up
the essence of Russian spirituality. The immediate impact of the
Gospels permeates it at all times. The use of the Slavonic language
in the Bible and at the celebration of a Mass gives it an original
Russian flavour. But to quote G. P. Fedotov again: 'kenoticism,
in the sense of charitable humility as well as of non-resistance, or
voluntary suffering, remains forever the most precious and
typical, even though not always the dominant, motif of Russian
Christianity.' Other writers have referred to the freedom of spirit,
the detachment from material goods, the love of pilgrimages.

There was always the consciousness of being a sinner. Hence the intense movement towards holiness for purification and transfiguration. The ideal towards which Russian spirituality tends is not one of well-being, but one of holiness. Always the example of Christ is held before the eyes. The two young princes already mentioned went even to martyrdom in order 'innocently to suffer the passion'.

Russian spirituality sank to a low ebb in the eighteenth century. Renewal began in 1825 when Saint Seraphim of Sarov opened the door of his cell and inaugurated the era of the 'Staretz'. In the figure of Zosima in *The Brothers Karamazov*, Dostoevsky has depicted the first known representative of this class of spiritual elders.

St Seraphim

St Seraphim is the most influential and highly regarded Orthodox saint of the last two centuries. He was born in 1759. On the evening of 20 November 1778 he crossed the threshold of the monastery of Sarov. In 1793 Seraphim, then aged thirty-four, received priestly ordination. From then on he celebrated the liturgy daily. It was, for him, 'a well of water springing up into everlasting life'. He had long felt called by the 'desert'.

In 1794, when he was thirty-five he obtained permission to go and 'rest' as the wording on his permit put it. This meant achieving the solitude of the forest. We are told by his biographer Valentina Zandor that he seemed prematurely aged. He was weakened by sickness and fasting and his legs were swollen and covered with sores. He went through horrible experiences under the assault of the devil. 'He who has chosen the hermit life,' he said later, 'must feel himself constantly crucified. . . . The hermit, tempted by the spirit of darkness, is like dead leaves chased by the wind, like clouds driven by the storm; the demon of the desert bears down on the hermit at about mid-day and sows restless worries in him, and distressing desires as well. These temptations can only be overcome by prayer.'

He was beaten up by three bandits in search of his non-existent treasure. His convalescence lasted several months. His hair turned white. He remained a hunchback for the rest of his life. He embarked on a further degree of asceticism – that of silence – but when it was discovered by his superiors that he was no longer receiving communion in his hermitage he was induced to return to the monastery after 15 years of the solitary life. After five years of strict enclosure the time came when he no longer 'kept his doors shut.' Soon visitors began to pour in, not only young monks and novices but superiors from neighbouring monasteries as well. When a visitor entered he would give him the kiss of peace and if it were a priest or a superior of the monastery he would prostrate himself before him. He became a 'Staretz', famous far and wide. He was by no means the first staretz but he might well be described as the most illustrious. The tradition of startzi has been described correctly as a characteristic phenomenon of the Orthodox Church, though not an official institution. Tolstoi wrote: 'If the Russian people have still preserved the true image of the living Christ, it is only among the startzi that they have done so.'

Vladimir Lossky, in his classic work, *The Mystical Theology of the Eastern Church*, refers to the startzi in this way. 'These are most frequently monks who, having passed many years of their life in prayer and secluded from all contact with the world, towards the end of their life throw open to all comers the door of their cell.' He attributes to them the gift of directing men not only in their spiritual course but also 'in all the vicissitudes in their lives in the world'. In the case of Father Seraphim the silence and enclosure were only the prelude to this period. 'When, at over sixty years of age, Seraphim came to devote himself to suffering humanity and to spend the rest of his life besieged by crowds who came to him seeking his help and comfort' (Zandor).

There is a strong tradition that Czar Alexander I visited Father Seraphim about 1825. It is an historical fact that Alexander soon afterwards abandoned the throne and lived in Siberia until 1864 under the name of Staretz Fedor Kuzmitch. It is also known that the Imperial family remained devoted to Seraphim long after his death. The wife of Czar Nicholas I said on her death bed, 'I am sure that this little old man will help me to die well.' Seraphim's cloak was sent to her from Sarov. Wrapped in it she passed away peacefully.

I need not continue the story of Seraphim's life except to mention the fact that he kept leaving the monastery to return to the forest. He underwent trials of various kinds in spite of and because of his acknowledged sanctity. His fatherly concern for a community of nuns produced much jealous criticism. But there was overwhelming recognition of his holiness. He died in 1832 (?) aged 73.

I must turn briefly to his message. An intense joyfulness permeated everything said and done by Saint Seraphim along with continuous sufferings. In a theological sense he is most famous for his profound teaching regarding the Holy Spirit. Here it is necessary to refer to the deepest reason for the split between the Eastern and Western Churches. Vladimir Lossky explicitly rejects the attempt to treat the division as primarily political or social, racial or cultural. 'If we consider,' he writes, 'the dogmatic question of the procession of the Holy Spirit, which divided East and West, we cannot treat it as a fortuitous phenomenon in the history of the Church. From the religious point of view it is the sole issue of importance in the chain of events which terminated in the separation. Conditioned, as it may well have been, by various factors, this dogmatic choice was – for the one party as for the other – a spiritual commitment, a conscious taking of sides in a matter of faith.'

Putting the matter crudely the Holy Spirit occupies a much more significant position in the Eastern than in the Western Church. In the Western Church the Holy Spirit proceeds from the Father and the Son, in the Eastern Church directly from the Father. Enormous theological consequences follow which cannot be spelt out here. Lossky tells us that the two traditions have separated 'on a mysterious doctrinal point relating to the Holy Spirit who is the source of holiness. . . . Since the separation, the ways which lead to sanctity are not the same in the West as in the East. The one proves its fidelity to Christ in the solitude and abandonment of the night of Gethsemane, the other gains certainty of union with God in the light of the Transfiguration.'

Saint Seraphim did not create the Eastern tradition but he renewed it most potently and expounded it with unique force among modern spiritual leaders. Lossky writes at length about the resulting 'gnosis' or consciousness of union with God. He quotes various sayings of Saint Seraphim as illustrating the nature of the certainty and its relationship to the doctrine of the Holy Spirit. On one occasion Saint Seraphim said to his disciple 'my friend we are both at this moment in the spirit of God. Why won't you look at me?' The disciple replied 'I can't look at you Father. Your eyes shine like lightning. Your face has become more dazzling than the sun.'

Suffering and joy are the twin pillars of Russian spirituality. Michael Bourdeaux, in his book *Risen Indeed* describes in moving terms the celebration of Easter in Moscow in recent years: 'Every one of the worshippers held a candle. In less than a minute the church was a blaze of light – no, not the impersonal glare of electricity – it was five thousand individual flames united in one faith. Each candle lit up a face behind it. That face bore the deep lines of sorrow, of personal tragedy. Yet as it was illuminated, the suffering turned to joy, to the certain knowledge of the reality of the risen Lord.' As Michael Bourdeaux remarks so convincingly: 'They have trodden the way of the Cross to the hill of Calvary . . . they have not preserved the faith in hostile surroundings, it has preserved them. Their joy is truly a glimpse through the curtain which divides us from Heaven.' Truly the spirit of Saint Sergius and St Seraphim is as much alive today as when they first exhibited their total commitment to Christ.

Part II
OTHER MEN OF GOD

18

MARTIN LUTHER
1483–1546

Luther's impact on the world was enormous, for good or for ill. In sheer magnitude it ranks with that of Napoleon, Karl Marx and Lenin – a sobering thought. To judge Luther without an attitude, favourable or unfavourable, to his achievement, seems almost impossible, not least for a Roman Catholic writer. 'The influence of Luther on mankind,' says H. A. L. Fisher, in his classic *History of Europe*, 'was not restricted to that German and Scandinavian area which was permanently won for the Lutheran Church, but penetrated everywhere. His bold challenge rang through Europe. Was it true that the world had been treading a false road for more than a thousand years, that the Papacy was an imposture, the special sanctity of priesthood a fiction, and that rites, ceremonies and institutions interwoven with the familiar life of Europe were unnecessary and even harmful? Only the dullest indifference could fail to be startled by such a message. Opinions might differ as to its value. Some might think it very good, others very wicked.' But no one could deny the excitement created. It was Luther who initiated the tremendous revolt. On the Continent and in England, where reform took a different shape, it was he who sowed the seed and prepared the ground.

Was the Reformation initiated by Luther the most enlightened or the most disastrous development in the religious history of the last thousand years? Many men of powerful intelligence have expressed both opinions. The present writer, a Roman Catholic, leans inevitably to the latter view, but it can be argued that it was a vehement assault on the Catholic Church as he found it that led to a lasting purification of that same Church. Today, the leaders of the Roman Catholic and Anglican Churches, and indeed most Christians of goodwill are aiming to restore Christian unity – in a sense therefore to undo the Reformation. The future is what matters now.

The first time that the name of Luther was brought home to me was when my Eton headmaster, Dr Cyril Alington, quoted the famous phrase about him: 'He was a God-intoxicated man.' But for many years afterwards, I never found anyone to tell me of Luther's relevance.

Luther was born at Eisleben (West Germany) in 1483. He died, also at Eisleben, in 1546. The best-known events in his career occurred in 1517 and 1521. On the first occasion, he pinned ninety-five theses against Papal indulgences to the door of the Castle Church at Wittenberg. On the second occasion he stood up before the Imperial Diet and said (as far as can be ascertained): 'Here I stand, I can do no other.'

His parents belonged to the free peasant class; his father found employment as a miner. When he was thirteen, Martin was sent to Magdeburg to complete his education and, in accordance with the practice at the time, earned his bread by singing in the streets. He was soon picked out as a boy of exceptional promise. In 1501, that is, in his eighteenth year, he entered the University of Erfurt, at that time in the front rank of German universities. By the time he passed his Master's examination, second in a list of seventeen candidates, he had studied grammar, logic, rhetoric, physics, mathematics and ethics. In due course he became steeped in Cicero, Virgil and Livy.

In 1505, he suddenly renounced the world and entered the monastery of the Augustinian Eremites at Erfurt to the dis- appointment of his father who had intended him for the law. He was ordained a priest in 1507. He continued to study intensively. In 1511 he was transferred to the monastery of Wittenberg. A year later he took the degree of Doctor of Theology and became, in due course, a professor. By the time he was thirty, he was powerfully equipped as an intellectual theologian.

In 1510 he had paid a short visit to Rome. He was not favourably impressed but his hostility had not yet formed. Now came his conversion. He had become more and more unhappy and guilt-ridden as time went on. Prayer, fasting and scourging brought him no peace, nor lightened his agonising burden of imputed sin. He saw the abject wickedness of Man, himself of course included, and against it the infinite but unapproachable goodness of God. Where could a bridge be found?

The story is best told in his own words: 'I greatly longed to understand Paul's Epistle to the Romans and nothing stood in the way but that one expression, "the justice of God". I took it to mean that justice whereby God is just and deals justly in punishing the unjust. My situation was that, although an impeccable monk, I stood before God as a sinner troubled in conscience, and I had no confidence that my merit would assuage him. Therefore I did not love a just and angry God, but rather hated and murmured against him. Yet I clung to dear Paul and had a great yearning to know what he meant.'

Luther pondered night and day until he saw the connection between the justice of God and the statement that the just shall live by His faith. 'Then I grasped that the justice of God is that righteousness by which, through grace and sheer mercy, God justifies us through faith. Thereupon I felt myself to be reborn and to have gone through open doors into paradise. The whole of Scripture took on a new meaning, and whereas before the "justice of God" had filled me with hate, now it became to me inexpressibly sweet in greater love. This passage of Paul became to me a gate to heaven. If you have a true faith that Christ is your saviour your faith leads you in and opens up God's heart and will so that you see pure grace and overflowing love.'

It has been well pointed out by Rowland Bainton, whose book *Here I Stand* is the best English biography of Luther, that Luther's new insights contained already the marrow of his mature theology. The salient ideas were present in the lectures on Psalms and Romans from 1513 to 1516. What came after was but commentary and sharpening to obviate misconstruction. Was the new theological message bound to lead to the traumatic quarrel with the Catholic Church and the break-up of the unity of Christians? I cannot see that it was inevitable from the beginning, though as time went on the breach became irrevocable. Take, for example, the concept of justification by faith. Brought up as a Protestant in the Church of Ireland, I cannot now recall having heard the phrase, though I suppose it was mentioned in the historical context. Certainly it was never an element in any Christian teaching that I received then or later in my Anglican days.

In August 1986 a learned controversy took place in *The Tablet* regarding justification by faith. I find myself convinced by the views of Dr Edward Yarnold, SJ, a member of the Anglican–

Roman Catholic Commission since its beginning. He points out that the Anglican 'Communion as such is not committed to the Reformation doctrine of justification, however much the evangelical party within it may be. He concludes, 'that one cannot accept without extensive qualification the view that the fundamental divide between the two traditions in the sixteenth century concerned the doctrine of justification.'

One cannot help thinking that if Luther had been handled more wisely by the Catholic Church, a great tragedy and an historic split could have been averted. It has been suggested to me by a wise priest that there is a considerable feeling of guilt in the Catholic Church today about the treatment of Luther, before he seceded. If that is so, it is by no means unreasonable. Be that as it may, one returns to the question of why the doctrine of justification by faith led inevitably to the public attack on indulgences and all that followed. We must try to put ourselves in the position of deeply committed Christians who were horrified by some prominent aspects of the Catholic Church at that time, the system of indulgences being a glaring example.

The idea that the Pope could issue indulgences for the remittance of sins was rooted in the theory that there had been accorded to St Peter and his successors an inexhaustible treasury of merit. The treasury was originally due to the sacrifices of Christ, but it was continually augmented by successive generations of believing Christians. It was a short step to the selling of indulgences for the benefit of the living and the dead in order to meet the pecuniary needs of the popes. No Catholic today would defend such a system. Few would deny that it represented an element of human corruption in the Catholic Church of the sixteenth century. To Luther the system was particularly repulsive. The immediate object of his attack was the declared intention of the papacy to raise money in order to shelter the bones of St Peter in a universal shrine of Christendom. Luther retorted: 'The revenues of all Christians are being sucked by this insatiable Basilica. . . . Why doesn't the Pope build the Basilica of St Peter out of his own money? He is richer than Croesus. He would do better to sell St Peter's and give the money to the poor folk who are being fleeced by the hawkers of indulgences.'

On the eve of All Saints 1517, Luther posted on the door of the Castle Church in Wittenberg a printed placard in Latin consisting

of ninety-five theses for debate. There was nothing unusual in posting a placard on the church door: this was the recognised way of establishing a debate. But the tone of the theses caused a sensation. 'Papal indulgences do not remove guilt. Beware of those who say that indulgences effect reconciliation with God. The power of the keys cannot make attrition into contrition. He who is contrite has plenary remission of guilt and penalty without indulgences. The Pope can remove only those penalties which he himself has imposed on earth, for Christ did not say "Whatsoever I have bound in heaven you may loose on earth".' The penalties of purgatory the Pope could not reduce because these have been imposed by God. The Pope did not have at his disposal a treasury of credits available for transfer.

Even after the posting of the theses, Luther continued to see himself as and, on the whole, behave like a loyal Catholic. In February 1518 he submitted his theses to his diocesan bishop, with the request that he should strike out anything in them that appeared to be offensive: if he pleased let him throw the whole manuscript into the fire. Luther wished everything in the enclosed pages to be regarded as merely provisional, disputable opinion. He repeatedly emphasised his absolute submission to the direction of the Holy See. But it was perhaps too much to hope that such apparent defiance could be handled with kindness and tolerance.

The Pope is supposed to have remarked at an early stage: 'Friar Martin is a brilliant chap. The whole row is due to the envy of the monks.' But the pressures on him, especially from the Dominicans, achieved their effect. In 1519 there was a famous disputation at Leipzig between Luther and the theologian Eck. The description of Luther by a professor of poetry present at the encounter brings Luther before us: 'Martinus is of middle height emaciated from care and study so that you can almost count all his bones through his skin. But he is in the vigour of manhood, his voice rings clear and distinct. He has the Scriptures by heart and commands sufficient Greek and Hebrew. A perfect forest of ideas and words is at his command. He is affable and friendly, not a bit austere or arrogant. In company he is vivacious, jocose, always cheerful and gay. Everyone chides him for being a little too insolent in his strictures and more caustic than is prudent or becoming.' In the course of the debate, Luther was drawn on to carry his doctrine further and further in a radical direction, contravert the divine right of the Papacy and assert the supreme authority of scripture. There was little room for negotiation left.

In January 1521, the Pope, in consequence of Luther's refusal to retract and submit to the authority of the Church, launched a Bull of Excommunication and called on the Emperor Charles V to execute it forthwith. The Emperor summoned Luther to appear for examination before the Diet, sitting at Worms. Luther was called on to recant. In reply he requested to be convinced of his error from scripture. Being further pressed, he uttered the historic words: 'Unless I am convinced by scripture or by an evident reason [*ratione evidente*] – for I confide neither in the Pope nor in a council alone, since it is certain that they have often erred and contradicted themselves – I am held fast by the Scriptures adduced by me, and my conscience is taken captive by God's word and I neither can nor will revoke anything, seeing that it is not safe or right to act against conscience. God help me. Amen.' It is traditional and reasonable to assume that at this point he added the words 'Here I stand, I can do no other. God help me. Amen.'

There was no hope for conciliation thereafter. By this time one must think of Luther as a representative of a tremendous protest throughout Germany and beyond. To quote H. A. L. Fisher again: 'He was a self-experiencing religious genius who in his search for personal salvation was led by degrees to take up an attitude which made him the champion of the German nation against the claims of the Roman Church. . . . All the strength, all the weakness of the German character was reflected and magnified in his passionate temperament, his tenderness and violence, his coarseness in vituperation and old-fashioned biblical piety.'

In 1524 came the Peasants' Revolt, which is rightly looked upon as providing the most serious blot on Luther's record. Luther took the side of the Princes and Lords and issued what can only be called an appeal for a war of extermination against the rebels. If there were any question of Luther being officially treated as a saint, the Devil's Advocate would be able to use his attitude to the Peasants' Revolt in deadly fashion.

Diets came and went. That which met at Spires in 1526 carried a resolution not unfavourable to Luther. That of Augsburg in 1530 saw Luther's lieutenant, Melanchthon, presenting a confession of the Lutheran faith, but it did not succeed. Luther at last overcame his scruples and was ready to support active resistance to the imperial authority in defence of the evangelical cause.

His theology continued to develop. In Luther's maturity, the crucial change was from the Mass to the Lord's Supper. This was much more than a matter of words. Luther insisted, contrary to Catholic teaching, that the efficacy of the sacrament of the Holy Communion depended upon the faith of the recipient. 'I may be wrong on the indulgences,' declared Luther, 'but as to the need for faith in the sacrament, I will die before I recant.' It followed that he much diminished the role of the priest. Yet Luther insisted to the end, unlike other reformers who went far beyond him, that God was indeed present in the body and blood through the sacrifice on the Cross made once for all. The sacrament, according to Luther, does not conjure up God, but reveals Him where He is. The role of the clergyman remained significant, though not dominating, as he considered that of the priest in traditional Catholicism.

Luther lived another sixteen years, but as Rowland Bainton observes, 'they are commonly treated more cursorily by biographers than the earlier periods, if indeed they are not omitted altogether'. He acknowledges that 'the last quarter of Luther's life was neither determinative for his ideas nor crucial for his achievement'. Two aspects, however, cannot be passed over altogether. In 1525 Luther married; in due course he had six children. He summed up his reasons for marriage: to please his father, to spite the Pope and the Devil and to seal his witness before martyrdom.

There is something disarming, if chauvinistic, about his attitude. To one friend he wrote: 'You must come to my wedding. I have made the angels laugh and the Devil weep.' To another: 'Undoubtedly the rumour of my marriage must have reached you. I can hardly believe it myself, but the witnesses are too strong.' He maintained the devotion of his wife, Katherine von Bora, a nun who had been left to work in domestic service when, under Luther's influence, she abandoned the cloister. One of his characteristic comments was: 'All life is patience. I have to have patience with the Pope, the heretics, my family and Katy.' But there is no doubt that Luther was happy and much loved in his home.

Of lasting significance to the world was his translation of the Bible, often referred to as the noblest of all his works. Justification by faith alone, emphasised in St Paul, appears to be denied in the

Epistle of St James. In Luther's preface to the New Testament of
1522, the Epistle of James was stigmatised as 'an epistle of straw'.
Once he remarked that he would give his doctor's beret to anyone
who could reconcile James and Paul. 'Faith,' he also wrote, 'is a
living, restless thing. It cannot be inoperative. We are not saved by
works, but if there be no works, there must be something amiss
with faith.'

It is frequently claimed that no man has done so much to shape
the character of the German people. Bainton says: 'Their
language was so far fashioned by his hand that the extent of their
indebtedness is difficult to recognise. . . . The most profound
impact of Luther on his people was on their religion. His sermons
were read to the congregations, his liturgy was sung, his catechism
was rehearsed by the father with his household, his Bible cheered
the faint-hearted and consoled the dying.' Something similar can
be claimed for Cranmer in England, though not surely on the same
scale.

If we try to measure Luther on the scale of modern values, we
have to recognise that he did not believe in free enquiry or
toleration; he held firmly to the belief that all truth as to the
ultimate problems of life and mind was to be found in Holy Writ.
It may indeed be true that Luther's appeal to the so-called modern
mind is strictly limited. It seems fair however to end with a
quotation from the present Pope.

Speaking to the evangelical church at Mainz on 16 November
1980, the Pope showed an expert knowledge of Luther's life and of
the Epistle to the Romans which Luther has described as the heart
of the New Testament. 'We have all,' said the Pope, 'in the spirit of
Luther sinned. We cannot therefore judge each other. Jesus Christ
is the salvation of us all. Through him the Father grants us
pardon, justification, grace and eternal life. We must all confess
these truths.' We are told that the evangelical churchmen were left
uncertain as to what, if any, difference remained between the
Pope's approach to Luther and their own. Perhaps as the years
pass, that difference will seem smaller and smaller.

19
CARDINAL NEWMAN
1801–1890

Four years before he became Prime Minister, Lord Rosebery wrote a description of the dead Newman that haunts my memory: 'Seeing him there in outline only, I saw only an enormous nose and chin, a Saint Dominic face. The left side was inconceivably sweet and soft, with the gentle drooping of the mouth, so greatly missed in the other view. . . . So this was the end of the young Calvinist, the Oxford don, the austere vicar of St Mary's. It seemed as though a whole cycle of human life and thought were concentrated in that august repose. . . . Kindly Light had led a guided Newman to that strange, brilliant, incomparable end.'

The interest in John Henry Newman seems to grow and grow. No other religious writer of the last century, except perhaps Saint Teresa of Lisieux, has acquired so wide a following. In the last forty years knowledge and love of Cardinal Newman have spread all over the world. Monsignor Stark, the high authority in charge of the Cause of his canonisation during its diocesan process, tells me that the last visitors' book at Birmingham Oratory recorded signatures from eighty-six different nations. Two remarkable additions have appeared in the current book: Afghanistan and Czechoslovakia. Among the many high-ranking visitors are several cardinals and archbishops. At Littlemore, several hundred visitors have initialled the visitors' book expressing their desire to see Newman canonised. Among these are Cardinals Pellegrino, Suenens, Knox and Wright. Another, Cardinal Morella, arch-priest of St Peter's, remarked to Father Humphrey of the Oratory: 'You have only to read his books to see he was a saint.' The Cause itself was formally opened in 1958 by the late Archbishop Grimshaw of Birmingham.

In summer 1986, his Cause was presented to Rome by the Birmingham (Catholic) archdiocese, with the fervent support of the whole hierarchy of England and Wales. The battle is not over yet. It is likely, however, that Newman will be beatified in the not too near future and canonised in due course.

In an address on Newman Cardinal Hume has told us: 'I have wondered whether he was a fit subject for canonisation. A holy person is canonised only if he or she gives evidence of heroic sanctity. I never doubted his holiness or his greatness. But heroism? It was on this point that I hesitated. Now I think that I was wrong.' He went on to say that he had been influenced decisively by the views of Pope John Paul I. In a letter to Archbishop Dwyer on 7 April 1979 the present Pope wrote thus: 'I wish to express my personal interest in the process for beatification of this "good and faithful servant" of Christ and the Church. I shall follow with close attention whatever progress may be made in this regard.'

The Pope spoke also of Newman's:

deep intellectual honesty;
fidelity to conscience and grace;
policy and priestly zeal;
devotion to Christ's Church and love of doctrine;
unconditional trust in divine providence;
absolute obedience to the will of God.

John Henry Newman was born in the City of London on 21 February 1801. His father was a partner in the banking house of Ramsbottom, Newman & Co; his mother belonged to a well-known Huguenot family. John Henry was the eldest of six children. We are indebted to his autobiography, *Apologia Pro Vita Sua*, for much knowledge of his early life. From childhood he was brought up to take great delight in reading the Bible. He dates his 'inward conversion' to the autumn of 1816, when he was fifteen. 'I fell under the influence of a definite creed and received into my intellect impressions of dogma which have never been effaced or obscured.' The religious literature which he read at this time, however, was chiefly Calvinist. He became firmly convinced that the Pope was the anti-Christ predicted by Daniel, St Paul and St John.

When still just under sixteen, he entered Trinity College, Oxford, and two years later gained one of the Trinity scholarships. In 1819 financial crisis struck his family when the bank in which his father was a partner stopped payment.

His collapse in the final Schools was disappointing. Instead of the brilliant first-class degree predicted, his name was found 'below the line' in the second division of the second class of honours. Every kind of explanation has been offered, including overwork. He was not then twenty, whereas the usual age for graduating was twenty-two, and had clearly been pushed ahead much too fast.

Showing the resolution in the face of adversity which was never to desert him, he fought back academically. On 12 April 1822 he was elected a fellow of Oriel – the equivalent these days to a fellowship at All Souls. This day he 'ever felt to be the turning-point of his life and of all days most memorable'. It gave him the inner confidence essential to such a sensitive man. His intellectual life went forward hand in hand with his spiritual life. He became an Anglican priest in 1825 and Vicar of St Mary's, the Oxford university church, in 1828. He would resign from St Mary's fifteen years later on his way to Rome.

'There is no need,' to quote Monsignor Stark again, 'to detail Newman's career as a fellow, as a tutor, as curate of St Clement's, or his distinguished service to the university and the City of Oxford as Vicar of St Mary's, when the church would be packed every Sunday to hear those wonderful sermons, published under the title of *Parochial and Plain*. This was the time of Newman's greatest influence at Oxford . . .'. Indeed, the voice of this young clergyman, still in his twenties when appointed, echoed round England.

Dr Owen Chadwick, until recently Regius Professor at Oxford, says of these addresses which Newman was happy to republish in later years: 'Newman never wrote better, never more powerfully, never more persuasively. These books of sermons make the heart of that body of thought which came in history to be known as the mind of the Oxford Movement.'

What was the essence of that doctrine? 'Newman,' says Chadwick, 'studied – more than studied, he revered – the age of the early Christians. In his eyes, this was catholicity. Partly by lapse of time and partly by the weakness of men, there came incongruity between catholicity and the average English Protestantism of 1830. Newman aimed to screw the second up to the first. He was a true reformer.'

In the deepest sense Newman's spirituality retained the same character till the end of his days. His great gift of communicating his sense of the reality of the spiritual world and his personal vision of Christ never altered, though no doubt – to use his own words –they never ceased to develop. But his attitude to the Church of England and the Church of Rome was to be transformed. In his greatest days as an Anglican he found holiness in that Church, idolatry in the Church of Rome. Later he was to look upon the Roman Catholic Church as the one true Church. He never lost, however, his profound affection for the Church of England, which he was later to describe as the great bulwark against infidelity in England.

The time came when his immersion in the Early Fathers led him into some disconcerting discoveries affecting his confidence in the credentials of the Church of England. We need not go into them here. 'From the end of 1841,' writes Newman, 'I was on my death bed as regards my membership with the Anglican Church, though at the time I became aware of it by degrees.' A year later he withdrew from Oxford and took up his abode at Littlemore, close by, with several young men who had attached themselves to him. Here he passed three years of painful anxiety and suspense, leading a life of prayer, fasting and monastic seclusion. 'On the one hand,' he tells us, 'I gradually came to see that the Anglican Church was formally in the wrong; on the other the Church of Rome was formally in the right. Then that no valid reason could be assigned for continuing in the Anglican and again that no valid objection could be taken to joining the Roman.'

At the beginning of 1845, he began his *Essay on the Development of Christian Doctrine*, which he never finished. As he proceeded with his studies, his last doubts respecting the Roman Church disappeared. He was received in his house at Littlemore on 9 October 1845 by Father Dominic, a Passionist. Exactly half of Newman's life had passed. There was much unhappiness to follow, but never a moment's doubt whether he had taken the right course.

Following his reception into the Catholic Church and a period of re-education in Rome, he was installed as Head of the Oratory in Alcester Street, Birmingham, later in Edgbaston. In 1854 he went to Dublin at the invitation of the Irish Catholic bishops recently established there. But the enterprise proved a failure. On the other hand, Newman's volume on 'The Idea of a University' remains a classic. He was much occupied with a project for the establishment at Oxford of a branch house of the Oratory.

The project, however, came to nothing in consequence of the opposition of influential Catholics, including (Cardinal) Provost Manning. A scheme for a new English rendering of the Vulgate, which he took up at the suggestion of Cardinal Wiseman, also collapsed. In the early 1860s he could have been described without gross malevolence as a failure. It was twenty years since he had held the congregations at St Mary's spellbound.

In January 1864, Charles Kingsley, reviewing anonymously in Macmillan's magazine Froude's *History of England*, made the unfortunate comment: 'Truth for its own sake has never been a virtue with the Roman clergy; Father Newman informs us that it need not, and on the whole ought not to be.' Newman at once sprang into the fray, denouncing 'this grave and gratuitous slander'. A correspondence followed which culminated in Newman's sitting down to write his *Apologia*. The *Apologia*, Shane Leslie observed, marked the ebb of the Reformation in the English mind. Thenceforward anti-papal prejudice gradually ceased to be an indispensable passport to intellectual respectability.

The author of the article on Newman in the *Dictionary of National Biography* is surely correct in his verdict: 'It revolutionised the popular estimate of its author. From that time until his death, widely as most of his countrymen differed from his religious opinions, there was probably no living man in whose unswerving rectitude they more entirely believed, or for whom they entertained a greater reverence.'

Yet it was not until 1879, when the recently elected Pope Leo XIII appointed Newman a Cardinal, that Newman felt that the cloud over him had lifted. Monsignor Stark refers to the 'constant suspicion and misunderstanding' to which he was subjected by many of his fellow Catholics, even those in the highest positions in the Church.

Newman lived another eleven years after 1879, growing gradually weaker and more and more honoured by all.

Against this biographical background, how do we assess the performance and the man? Dr Chadwick passes this verdict: 'His work included friendliness to Protestants, assent to the place of history in the development of Christian thought, recognition of the free rights of critical enquiry, recognition that scientists are free to follow their arguments wherever they lead, antipathy to extremist forms of doctrine or devotion, confession that the great secret body of lay Christians was also the Church and not slaves of a hierarchy.'

Chadwick is disturbed by the fact that when Newman was installed as a cardinal, he insisted that his life's work had been an attempt to counter liberalism. Chadwick persuades himself that Newman's idea of liberalism was no one else's. Certainly Newman said on that occasion that liberalism was a habit of mind that treated one form of belief as being as good as another, and that led inevitably to indifferentism. But the liberalism which Newman devoted his life to countering seems to me to have been in a deeper sense what is often called rationalism – the attempt to arrive at ultimate religious truth by the use of human reason alone.

The outstanding quality of Newman's thinking, expressed through his literary genius, was to strike a balance between these two indispensable sources of knowledge – reason and revelation. It is impossible to say which of the two comes first at any moment. Newman's defection from the Church of England into the arms of Rome followed a devastatingly thorough investigation of the early Christian Fathers. As a source they must be placed under the heading of revelation rather than reason.

Once he became a Roman Catholic, his search for truth continued undiminished but always within a framework provided by Catholic teaching. He would never have publicly expressed a view in conflict with the official Catholic line, although he may privately have found a conflict between his own personal conclusions and the official pronouncements. We know that he was unhappy about the Vatican I announcement of the infallibility of the Pope. He did not, it would appear, question in his heart the rightness of the doctrine; he did criticise the wisdom of the timing. But here he himself had provided the means of psychological reconciliation. His own supreme intellectual achievement for me is the *Essay on the Development of Doctrine*. Mysteriously under the guidance of the Holy Spirit and functionally under the guidance of the Church, the development Newman defended was a movement towards a fuller grasp of truth. (Cf. *The Times*, Can Doctrine Develop?, 2 June 1986). Coupled with his sublime belief in divine providence, this view of things enabled him to feel that if he was unhappy with the teaching of the Catholic Church today, its teaching tomorrow or the day after could be relied on to put matters right. Pope Paul VI called Newman 'the doctor of Vatican

II'. Newman today is well entitled to feel that his perspective of a hundred years ago is fully justified.

There is much of Newman that cannot be touched on here. On his so-called holiday with Froude he wrote, after Froude left him in 1833, the most popular of all his verses, *Lead Kindly Light*, on an orange boat on the way to Marseilles from Palermo. He wrote the words of *The Dream of Gerontius*; he wrote *The Grammar of Assent* (1870). Sixty years later, Father Martin d'Arcy, SJ, seized on Newman's idea of the 'illative sense' as a means of arriving at knowledge in addition to the traditional methods of deduction and induction. Not only I, but many of my generation who were impatient of St Thomas's five proofs for the existence of God, found in the 'illative sense' a way of arriving at religious knowledge and belief through the accumulation of relevant evidence. So my personal debt to Newman must not go unrecorded.

Much has been said and much more remains to be said about Newman's holiness. Certainly he left an impression of holiness in his early years, which deepened in his later years. In 1882, the Lord Chief Justice of England, Lord Coleridge, tried to explain what he felt in Newman's presence: 'I cannot analyse it or explain it, but to this hour he interests and awes me like no other man I ever saw. He is as simple and humble and playful as a child and yet I am with a being unlike anyone else. He lifts me up for a time and subdues me – if I said frightens me, it would hardly be too strong; and if he does this to a commonplace old lawyer, what must he be to men who can really enter into him and feel with him!'

Father Philip Boyce, in a notable essay published by the Guild of Our Lady of Ransom, traces Newman's life-long search for holiness to his conversion in 1816: 'This deep change of thought sprang from a special awareness of God's presence. Whatever the exact circumstances were – and Newman is tantalizingly uninforming about them – the energetic and ambitious youth found himself at a certain moment confronted with Someone greater than himself. His proud intellect came up against a personal Lord, to whom he instinctively knew he had to submit.' The ensuing surrender in faith was his conversion. Louis Bouyer explains the confrontation as follows:

The young man, in the fullness of his intellectual pride and self-sufficiency, now becomes aware of something of some power, which he had dimly guessed at, even when he turned away from it. Something, someone, stronger and more wise than he, someone who subdued him to His will, even in the proudest hour of his intellectual self-reliance. To that other power, the mind, be it never so proudly confident, must needs defer. The very clearness with which he recognises this is a token that he has already surrendered.

The heart of his conversion is the gift of grace which we can only call a vivid awareness of God's presence. The famous phrase from the *Apologia*, 'myself and my Creator', arises from this inner consciousness of, and desire for, God that permeated Newman's life as a result of his conversion experience. And so it continued in the seventy-three years that followed.

But no one, except the Virgin Mary, has been perfect. Monsignor Stark, acknowledges: 'Newman was not without his faults. His character, for all its charm and attractiveness, has its weaknesses and oddities. He possessed a fine sensitivity, so much so that his detractors think that his Cause may fail on this subjective point, even if it surmounts all other obstacles.' Sensitivity sounds like an attractive quality but in an exaggerated form it clearly becomes a weakness.

Lytton Strachey, in his essay on Cardinal Manning, repeats the story told by Purcell, the most infelicitous biographer of the Cardinal. Manning had just delivered his marvellous funeral oration about Newman: 'We have lost our greatest witness to the faith and we are all poorer and lower for the loss.' Not long afterwards, Manning could not resist passing the comment: 'Poor Newman, he was a great hater.' Newman devotees will no doubt discount the truth of the story or the integrity of the alleged commentator.

Monsignor Stark suggests, not quite seriously perhaps, that 'only a saint could have effected the undoubted good Newman did, despite such a sensitive disposition.' The truth is that Newman, in the course of his life, Anglican and Catholic, was engaged in a good many unhappy personal relationships and not a few of what could be called quarrels in a less spiritual context. Most, if not all, of his adversaries in these disputes were men of high spiritual attitudes, even if those of Newman are to be judged higher still. Monsignor Stark (in the passage already quoted) refers to the 'constant suspicion and misunderstanding' to which Newman was subjected by many of his fellow Catholics, even those in the highest positions of the Church. But was that always entirely their fault? It seems very hard to think so. If so many religious people quarrelled with him, was it entirely due to the fact that they could not understand someone of a nature so superior to theirs? Newman showed a high degree of humility, however, and was totally sincere in his deference for over forty years to the Church of whose claims he was so passionate a champion.

Eight years after Newman became a cardinal, Bishop Ullathorne, his Ordinary, paid him a visit in the Oratory. Ullathorne wrote afterwards: 'We had a long and cheery talk, but as I was rising to leave an action of his caused a scene I shall never forget for its sublime lesson to myself.' Newman said in low and humble accents: 'My dear Lord, will you do me a great favour?' Ullathorne asked what it was. Newman glided down on his knees, bent down his venerable head and said: 'Give me your blessing.' 'What could I do with him before me in such a posture? I could not refuse without giving him great embarrassment. So I laid my hand on his head and said: "My dear Lord Cardinal, notwithstanding all laws to the contrary, I pray God to bless you, and that His Holy Spirit may be full in your heart." As I walked to the door, refusing to put on his biretta as he went with me, he said: "I have been indoors all my life, whilst you have battled for the Church in the world." I felt annihilated in his presence: there is a saint in that man!'

We are left asking the question, 'Was Newman a saint?' with considerable assurance that the answer will be and should be yes. He was in old age once asked bluntly: Which is greater – a cardinal or a saint? And replied, after a little thought: cardinals belong to this world and saints to Heaven. On another occasion, when it was suggested to him that he was a saint, he dismissed the issue with ridicule: 'I have nothing,' he said, 'of the saint about me as everybody knows. And it is a severe and salutary mortification to be thought next door to one. I may have a high view of many things, but it is the consequence of education and of a peculiar cast of intellect – but this is very different from *being* what I admire. . . . It is enough for me to black the saints' shoes – if St Philip uses blacking in Heaven.'

20

WILLIAM TEMPLE
1881–1944

When William Temple died in October 1944 at the age of sixty-three, a wave of shock and grief passed through the nation. He had only been Archbishop of Canterbury for two and a half years. Before that, he had been Archbishop of York for thirteen and, before that again, Bishop of Manchester for seven years. He was no stranger to national controversies and was associated, correctly, with left-wing sympathies. But from his broadcast at the outbreak of war he had become recognised increasingly as the moral conscience of the nation. He stood unequivocally for victory, but for a peace based on Christian principles.

Bishop Bell of Chichester, in a short memoir, wrote of 'his astonishing vitality, his many-sidedness, his all-embracing humanity, and his serene and humble faith. . .'. The grief and shock expressed themselves far beyond the borders of Britain. President Roosevelt cabled a message of sorrow to King George VI: 'As an ardent advocate of international co-operation based on Christian principles, Archbishop Temple exercised profound influence throughout the world.' Field-Marshal Smuts cabled: 'Church, nation and the world have suffered an irrefutable loss.' No one had done as much as Temple to promote the ecumenical movement, though during this period it was confined to the Protestant Churches. Temple's suspicion of the organised Roman Catholic Church will be touched on later. His personal friendliness to individual Roman Catholics was never in doubt.

He was a good, though not a great theologian. As I was writing these lines, a young man who has just taken his theological degree at Oxford told me that Temple is not today read for academic purposes. My young friend expressed much admiration for his *Readings in St John's Gospel* – as it happens a favourite of my own.

Temple was, however, unique among leaders of the Church of England in this century in having been as a young man a professional philosopher, Fellow and tutor in Queen's College, Oxford. (The present Pope, John Paul II, provides a parallel.) The rare combination of philosophy and theology brings to mind the supreme example of St Thomas Aquinas on whom, incidentally, I once heard Temple deliver a memorable lecture. The comparison with St Thomas, a stout man like himself, would have sent William Temple off into one of his famous explosions of rollicking laughter.

I am not thinking here of his world-wide influence, nor of his many-sided intellect, nor, for that matter, of his prodigious energy, affected though he was throughout his whole life by painful gout, and the fact that he could only use one eye for reading. I am thinking rather of two of the many tributes quoted by Canon Iremonger in the official *Life*. Early in 1944, Temple invited a small group from among the younger theologians for discussions at Canterbury. Some of them had come, it seems, feeling that they disagreed so fundamentally with Temple that they would be unable to say what they really thought; the opposite proved to be the case. One of them wrote afterwards: 'When we went away, we knew that we had been meeting with a man of prayer and a saint. That realisation overshadowed everything else. It was not his great intellect, or his astonishing gift of understanding, or the wideness of the theological rift, that made the deepest impression, but the fact of his holiness.'

When a Cumberland Dalesman heard of Temple's death, he shook his head and muttered sadly: 'He was a very *jolly* man.' That indeed I always found him, though not only that.

William Temple was born in October 1881. His father was Frederick Temple, then Bishop of Exeter, later Bishop of Fulham, finally Archbishop of Canterbury. His mother was of authentic aristocratic lineage – one of her grandfathers was the Earl of Harewood, the other the Earl of Carlisle. William was the second son. At the time of his birth, his father was fifty, his mother thirty-six, facts of significance to the dabbler in psychology. He adored them both. At Rugby he corresponded every week with his father and every day with his mother. His precocity of interest expressed in these letters is amazing. He cross-examined his father by letter on predestination and free will; on omnipotence and suffering; on Descartes (whose *Cogito, ergo sum* Temple had found more convincing since he had been 'thinking a little about

Brahminism'); on the scholastic philosophy, Butler's *Analogy* and Bacon's *Advancement of Learning* (the author, Temple notes, has considerable 'felicity of illustrating by image and metaphors' but is 'too metaphysical'); on the book of Ezekiel (then his favourite among the Prophets), the Epistle to the Hebrews (does his father agree that Apollos is as likely to have written it as anyone?), and Ecclesiastes (eight closely written sheets on the alleged 'pessimism' of the author); on a dozen other books, and above all on his father's Bampton Lectures, in which the Archbishop had presumed to criticise Kant, whose Categorical Imperative held his son under an early fascination.

One success followed another. 1895, Scholar of Rugby; 1900, Balliol College Exhibitioner; 1902, 1st Class Classical Moderations (his father died in this year). 1904, President of the Oxford Union; First Class *Literae Humaniores*; Fellow and Lecturer of Queens College, Oxford. 1909, ordained Priest by Archbishop of Canterbury (Randall Davidson). But here we must pause and glance at a rather out-of-character episode. In 1906 the Bishop of Oxford had turned down a tentative request for ordination from Temple on the ground that his views on the Prayer Book, virgin birth and the bodily resurrection were, to say the least, uncertain. Two years later Temple was able to satisfy the Archbishop of Canterbury that all was well. This seems to be the only occasion when Temple's career was positively assisted by his archiepiscopal background.

1910, Headmaster of Repton, aged twenty-nine (!); 1914, Rector of St James, Piccadilly. In the following year his mother died and in the year after that he married Francis Anson (the close sequence of events might again be of interest to the speculative psychologist). 1917–1921, leads movement for Christian Revival; then, as indicated above, 1921 Bishop of Manchester; 1929, Archbishop of York; 1942, Archbishop of Canterbury; 1944, 26 October, died at Westgate.

William Temple was so lavishly kind to so many men, women and children that I must not claim to have come closer than the periphery of his friendship. I first came under his spell when he spoke at Eton and the Headmaster, Dr Alington, asked a few of the sixth form to meet him privately. That would have been in 1923. By 1931 I felt I knew him well enough to consult him a week before I got married. I was still an Anglican of a sort. He gave me sage advice on birth control and other matters. During the war I stayed with him and Mrs Temple, a devoted couple. I can still remember the spasm of pain that passed over his face when I told him that I had become a Roman Catholic. I was not aware then that he had written some years earlier to a parish priest, 'I think that the people who are drawn to Rome are mostly people who would not be very valuable to the Church of England.' Canon Edward Carpenter in an essay on William Temple in his book about the Archbishop of Canterbury, speaks frankly of what Temple found 'uncongenial' in the ethos of the Roman Catholic faith. He quotes Temple as writing, 'I believe that all the doctrinal errors of Rome come from the direct identification of the Church as an organised institution, taking its part in the process of history, with the Kingdom of God.' Carpenter argues that Temple's attitude might have been considerably different after Vatican II. That seems a reasonable supposition, but there was always something very British about William Temple, for all his world-wide concern, and he may have found it difficult to shake off earlier preconceptions. Be that as it may, he treated me, after the initial surprise, with his habitual courtesy and eventually escorted me to the bus, limping painfully under his old enemy, the gout.

William Temple, although brought up with little contact with the working class, soon came to acquire a life-long sympathy with their aspirations. From 1908 to 1924, he was president of the Workers' Educational Association. For many years, he was a member of the Labour Party. Most of us continue to think of him as a member long afterwards, but he came to set a high value on being independent of party. During the miners' strike which followed the General Strike (1926), he landed himself in sharp controversy with Neville Chamberlain, then Conservative Minister of Health. His considered views on social questions can best be studied in his Penguin Special: *Christianity and Social Order* (1942). One paragraph gives a key to the rest: 'It is no part of the duty of a Christian as such to draw plans of a reformed society. But it is part of his duty to know and proclaim Christian principles, to denounce as evil what contravenes them, and to insist that those evils should be remedied. Further, it is his duty to judge how far particular evils are symptoms of a disease deeper than themselves, and if that seems to be so, to ask how far the whole existing order is contrary to the Natural Order.' A warm introduction to the new edition, published in 1976, was written by Edward Heath, recently Conservative Prime Minister.

Temple by no means confined himself to a statement of general principles. In a famous speech at the Royal Albert Hall on 26 September 1942, he provoked vehement controversy by a bold incursion into the field of banking. 'In my judgement at least – I don't claim that it is worth much, but I want to offer it to you – in my judgement at least it should now be regarded as improper for any private person or corporation to issue new credit; as it was in the Middle Ages for any private person or corporation to mint actual money, for the two are equivalent. And so I should like, I confess, to see the banks limited in their lending power to sums equivalent to that which depositors have entrusted to them, and all new credit to be issued by some public authority.' His attempts on this and other occasions to distinguish between his opinion as a private citizen and as Archbishop of Canterbury were unconvincing. Love of a good argument at times led him astray. Nevertheless, he was emerging as a national leader on social questions at just about the same time as my own chief Sir William, later Lord, Beveridge, an old friend of Temple's from Balliol days. Temple took the chair for Beveridge early in 1943 at a big public meeting after the publication of the historic Beveridge Report. Beveridge had got married at the end of 1942 to his cousin and long-term working partner Janet Mair, whose husband had just died. He hoped, as I did, that Temple would perform the marriage ceremony. There was no legal or theological objection to the marriage, but William Temple declined on the ground that Beveridge had not been, and did not propose to be, baptised. Temple did, however, perform a service of blessing, the marriage service itself being conducted in a Registry Office. Beveridge, resilient as always, assured me that 'it comes to the same thing'. I have sometimes thought that Temple was rather pernickety over this matter.

William Temple played a leading part in the reform of the educational system carried out in the Butler Act of 1944. The late Lord Butler described the part played by Temple in his usual idiosyncratical fashion: 'It was not he who took the main role in the reform of the Education Act of 1944, but until he gave me his help, all denominations were attacking my plan, particularly the Roman Catholics and High Anglicans, and without his assistance,

I might not have been successful. Temple's appointment to be Primate of All England was roundly condemned by the Conservatives at the time, as he had known socialist leanings, but Churchill wisely agreed that he should be translated from York to Canterbury. A genial and untidy person, all bulge and brain, he certainly had the best intellect among the Anglicans.'

But I have still not touched on what was the true source of his personal strength and all his manifold activities. He was filled with an overpowering love of Jesus Christ and just as overpowering a sense of evangelical vocation. For forty years, books, articles, sermons and lectures poured forth from him, mostly concerned with his Christian beliefs or their application to life. Nothing perhaps sums up William Temple's *credo* more vividly than this:

> Without Jesus Christ I can do nothing. All fruit that I ever bear or can bear comes wholly from His life within me. No particle of it is mine as distinct from His. There is, no doubt, some part of his whole purpose that He would accomplish through me; that is my work, my fruit, in the sense that I, and not another, am the channel of His life for this end; but in no other sense. Whatever has its ultimate origin in myself is sin; 'O God, forasmuch as without thee we are not able to please thee, mercifully grant that thy Holy Spirit may in all things direct and rule our hearts, through Jesus Christ our Lord.'

William Temple said more than once that he had never doubted the existence of God. The same was true of his attitude to the afterlife and the essentials of the Christian story. This simple, undisturbed piety, stemming initially from his beloved parents, was in one sense a weakness, and in another his greatest strength. It limited his understanding of the problems of those who found belief to be difficult or almost impossible. But his love of Christ overflowed directly and evidently into a love of men, women and children that won innumerable hearts. The weakness might have handicapped him still more in these times of still greater perplexity, but the strength might have led to his being valued and responded to still more widely.

21

MARTYRS OF THE TWENTIETH CENTURY

The early Christian saints, as mentioned earlier, were identical with the martyrs. In later centuries the categories have overlapped, but as with mysticism they are clearly distinguishable.

Two principal meanings are ascribed to the word martyr in the *Shorter Oxford Dictionary*: (1) a designation of honour for one who voluntarily undergoes the penalty of death for refusing to renounce the Christian faith or for obedience to any law or command of the Church; (2) one who undergoes death or great suffering on behalf of any belief or cause, or through devotion to some object. The second meaning is obviously too wide for our purpose. It would cover the countless men and women who laid down their lives for such causes as Nazism or Communism, causes which most readers will agree with me in finding disreputable. Even the holders of the Victoria Cross, whom we can wholeheartedly admire, are not what are usually called 'martyrs'. The first meaning broadly suits our purpose.

Twelve martyrs of the twentieth century are commemorated in the Martyrs' Chapel in Canterbury Cathedral, where Archbishop Runcie and Pope John Paul II placed lighted candles during the Pope's visit in 1982. Of the twelve men and women, three are Orthodox, three Roman Catholic, two Protestant and four Anglican. In this short survey, I will deal with six of the twelve who seem to me of special significance. My debt is obvious to Mary Craig, whose brilliant and moving book *Candles in the Dark* can be recommended without qualification. She reminds us not to forget the innumerable martyrs under Communist regimes. Of these six, four – Maximilian Kolbe, Archbishop Luwum, Maria Skobstova and Dietrich Bonhoeffer – were done to death in prison; two – Archbishop Romero and Martin Luther King – were assassinated in public.

Kolbe (1894–1941) we have already dealt with. *Archbishop Romero* (1917–1980) of San Salvador was considered by the authorities a sound man and generally looked upon as a conservative when he was appointed Archbishop early in 1977. Within eighteen months he had achieved world wide fame by his unrelenting protest at the way the government were carrying out a murderous persecution, in which the clergy suffered along with the mass of people. At the end of 1978, 118 Conservative members of the British parliament nominated him for the Nobel Peace Prize. He was well aware that his days were numbered. He said in his valedictory message:

> I have often been threatened with death. Nevertheless, as a Christian, I do not believe in death without resurrection. If they kill me, I shall rise again in the Salvadorean people. I say this in all humility without boasting.
>
> As a pastor, I am obliged by divine decree to give my life for those I love – for all Salvadoreans, even for those who may be about to kill me. If the threats come to be fulfilled, from this moment I offer my blood to God for the redemption and resurrection of El Salvador.

Later he insisted once again: 'If they succeed in killing me, I pardon and bless those who do the deed.' This note of forgiveness of the persecutors, and of loving one's enemies, is characteristic of those we shall be discussing.

Archbishop Romero was shot when saying Mass, soon after delivering the valedictory message. His successor immediately announced that he intended to petition for the beatification of Oscar Romero, who is already popularly regarded as a saint in Latin America. I have little doubt that he will in due course be canonised.

The Reverend Martin Luther King (1929–1968) presents us with a poignant problem. No one ever did more for the black community in America. No finer or more Christian message has ever been delivered that the one which, in one form or another, he preached continuously. He stood always for resistance to injustice and for the power of non-violence. 'Our aim must never be to defeat or humiliate the white man, but to win his friendship and under-standing. We must come to see that the end we seek is a society at peace with itself, a society that can live with its conscience. That will be a day not of the white man, not of the black man . . . that will be the day of man as man.'

Yet in one vital respect his life fell far below the Christian standards he inculcated. His relations with women were, to put it bluntly, scandalous. They provided his venomous enemy J. Edgar Hoover, Director of the FBI, with the evidence he needed to discredit King. Here, I disagree with Mary Craig. 'Saints, if we care to use the word at all,' she writes, 'can be seen struggling with their own weaknesses, like everyone else. What sets them apart is their vision and their readiness to lose everything, even their own lives, for the sake of that vision.' Beyond question, King had a glorious vision and laid down his life for the sake of it. In my eyes, however, to be a saint requires a degree of purity which in one area King was lacking. I feel confident that he would never have thought of himself in terms of sanctity. But he was a true martyr.

Maria Skobtsova (1891–1945), another heroic figure, had human weaknesses of a different kind. She was difficult to live with, and was twice divorced. When she became a nun, she was so unorthodox that she was once described as a 'walking offence'. She was frequently intolerant, except towards the poor and distressed.

Her life story is a remarkable tale. Brought up in a high position in Russia in the days of the Czars, she eventually made her way after the Revolution to Paris, where she devoted herself to caring for outcasts of all kinds. Eventually, during the German invasion, she was swept off and after hideous experiences found herself in a death cell. There she was remembered afterwards for her spiritual absorption and, at the same time, her unremitting care for fellow sufferers. It is not clear whether at the end, like Maximilian Kolbe, she took the place of a fellow victim in the ranks of those condemned to die, but such an act would have been entirely in character.

No character problems confront us in the case of *Archbishop Luwum* (1922–1977) of Uganda. The story of this Archbishop provides a close parallel with that of Archbishop Romero. If the Catholic Church did not confine canonisation to Roman Catholics, Archbishop Luwum would surely be a strong candidate. Already the Anglican Church has done him special honour. It was his murder in 1977 which prompted the Dean and Chapter of Canterbury Cathedral to set aside a chapel commemorating the saints and martyrs of our own times.

Like Archbishop Romero, Luwum found himself the leader of a Church under persecution, in a state where the persecution spread far and wide. The problem of how far to speak out and how far to try to conciliate the rulers was acute. Like Romero, he came down unhesitatingly on the side of uninhibited criticism but always, like Romero, he remained the complete Christian in his love of his enemies.

On one occasion, his house was invaded by soldiers demanding to know where the arms were stored, or to be told the names of those who were hiding them. Then as always the Archbishop was firm and yet charitable. 'This house,' he told the gunmen, 'is a house of prayer. The only armament I possess is the Bible. I pray for the President. I pray for you that you may learn to rule Uganda without destroying it.' Like Romero and Martin Luther King, he knew precisely where his bold stand was taking him. He was told by an official that the President wanted to see him. He rose to his feet and smiled at the Bishop with him: 'There is something I have not told you,' he said. 'Three days ago a girl came to warn me that I was number one on the security forces' death list. She had overheard some of the men talking in Swahili about it. She wanted me to escape, but I told her: "I cannot. I am the Archbishop. I must stay." ' He was never seen again.

The German *Dietrich Bonhoeffer* (1906–1945) was a man of immense intellect, in addition to his religious qualities. His end, after two years of imprisonment by the Nazis, was indubitably glorious. The prison doctor has left impressions which cannot be quoted too often:

> Through the half-open door in one of the huts I saw Father Bonhoeffer, before taking off his prison garb, kneeling on the floor, praying fervently to his God. I was most deeply moved by the way this lovable man was praying, so devoutly and so sure that God heard him. At the place of execution he again said a short prayer and then climbed the steps to the gallows, brave and composed. His death ensued after a few seconds. In the almost fifty years I worked as a doctor, I hardly ever saw a man die so submissive to the will of God.

During his imprisonment he had suffered from many painful anxieties. He was uncertain about his powers of resistance. From his prison notes we are aware that at one point he contemplated suicide. It was not surprising that at times he questioned his motives, after all, he was a Lutheran pastor, yet he had been deeply involved in the plot to assassinate Hitler and in the endless lies and subterfuges which derived from that objective. His course of action was repugnant to the Lutheran tradition of respect for the head of state and to non-violent idealism.

By the end it would seem that he had cleared his conscience and a great calm had descended. In his last letter he wrote:

> You must never doubt that I'm travelling with gratitude and cheerfulness along the road where I'm being led. My past life is brim ' full of God's goodness, and my sins are covered by the forgiving love of Christ crucified. I'm most thankful for the people I have met, and I only hope that they never have to grieve about me, but that they too will always be certain of, and thankful for God's mercy and forgiveness. . . .

The present writer finds it difficult to go the whole way with those who would like to canonise Bonhoeffer. There are passages in the *Letters from Prison*, those for example where he shows a certain contempt for prisoners unable to stand the strain, which do not make pleasant reading. The *Letters from Prison* are frequently said to have had great influence on subsequent theology, for instance, they would seem to have had such an influence on Bishop John Robinson, whose *Honest to God* startled the world of religion in the 1960s. But today the admirers of Bonhoeffer spend much of their time in explaining away the misunderstandings which seem to have arisen from Bonhoeffer's famous demand for a religionless Christianity. I am not aware that his influence is still powerful in Great Britain or Ireland. I cannot myself feel that it has been of positive value.

So of the six martyrs considered here, one, Father Kolbe, is a canonised saint. I presume to prophesy that the same honour will be accorded Archbishop Romero. The other four, not being Roman Catholics, are not eligible at the moment. But Archbishop Luwum would seem to stand on the same footing morally speaking as Archbishop Romero. Maria Skobtsova, Martin Luther King and Dietrich Bonhoeffer were heroic figures; the last two in particular have inspired vast numbers of Christians and indeed non-Christians by the way they lived and died.

22

THE SAINT IN MODERN LITERATURE

Out of a multitude of possibilities I have selected four writers to illustrate the idea of sanctity to be found in modern literature. The four chosen authors are: Dostoevsky (Orthodox); T. S. Eliot (Anglican); Graham Greene and Evelyn Waugh (both Roman Catholics).

Dostoevsky

Dostoevsky produced two and perhaps three models of Christian sanctity: in the hero of *The Idiot* and in *The Brothers Karamazov*, Father Zossima and possibly Aloysha, the youngest of the three brothers. 'There can be no doubt,' writes David Magarshack, editor and translator of *The Idiot*, that in *The Idiot* 'Dostoevsky has successfully attempted to present the ideal of a Christian.' The word 'successfully' is open to argument, but it is clear that in Prince Myshkin, the so-called idiot, Dostoevsky presents his idea of a perfect man. By most standards what a strange version of perfection!

When we first meet Prince Myshkin, he has just returned to Russia from many years of medical treatment abroad for epilepsy and nervous trouble. As the book proceeds, it is obvious that he is far from cured. He is loved by all discerning people, but soon acquires the soubriquet of Idiot. When he wants to marry a young beauty, her mother regards the prospect with horror. The engagement breaks down. The Prince, from a mixture of emotions, becomes engaged to a loose woman, also beautiful. At the door of the church she disappears with her previous lover. The Prince follows them only to find that he has murdered her. The lover forces the Prince to spend an extraordinary night in the next room to the murdered woman.

When the police arrive in the morning, both men are off their heads, the Prince it would seem permanently. The mother of the young beauty visits him in his clinic, but he does not begin to recognise her. His role, in a worldly sense, has been disastrous for himself and others. Yet Dostoevsky is confident that the purity of the Prince's motives and conduct demonstrates that he is as near as a human being can be to perfection. He loves everyone without thought of self. When he is about to marry the loose woman, the following dialogue takes place:

'Then, for heaven's sake, Prince, what are you doing?' Radomsky cried in dismay. 'So you're marrying her out of a sort of fear? I simply can't understand it! You're not even in love with her, perhaps?'

'Oh no, I love her with all my soul! Why, she's just a – a child, an absolute child! Oh, you know nothing!'

'And at the same time, you swore to Aglaya that you loved her?'

'Oh yes, yes!'

When, as mentioned just now, people discovered him alone with the murderer, they found the murderer completely unconscious and in a raging fever. 'The Prince was sitting motionless beside him on the cushions, and every time the sick man burst out screaming, or began rambling, he hastened to pass his trembling hand over his hair and cheeks, as though caressing and soothing him. But he no longer understood the questions he was asked, and did not recognise the people who had come into the room and surrounded him.' Conscious or unconscious, sane or gravely disturbed, Myshkin remains in Dostoevsky's eyes the incarnation of goodness.

Father Zossima, the Russian monk in *The Brothers Karamazov*, expresses in a different way the special kind of Christian virtue that appealed so much to Dostoevsky. Humility lies at the root of it. Father Zossima had been a young officer in a crack regiment who provoked a duel with a brother officer. The night before the encounter he returned home in 'an ugly and ferocious mood, lost his temper with his batman and slapped his face so hard that it was covered with blood'. By the next morning he was overwhelmed with remorse. In the duel, his opponent 'had the first shot'. 'I stood facing him, looking happy, without batting an eyelid. I looked at him lovingly, for I knew what I was going to do. He fired and just grazed my cheek and ear. "Thank God," I cried, "you haven't killed a man!" I seized my pistol, turned round and, flinging it high into the air, threw it into the wood. "That's the place for you!" I cried. Then I turned to my opponent and said:

"Forgive a stupid young fellow, Sir, for having insulted you without any provocation on your part and now forcing you to shoot at him. I'm ten times worse than you, and perhaps even more so." '

After that it was a short transition to his becoming a monk. It is no surprise to find him many years later preaching a message of universal sympathy for everyone in the world, especially those who depart this life in solitude, unknown to anyone, in anguish and sorrow.

Aloysha is a kind of Prince Myshkin without his mental affliction. He is persuaded to visit another of these beautiful loose women. She is determined to seduce him, resentful of his superior virtue. She suddenly springs up and jumps laughing on to his knee, 'like an affectionate kitten', flinging her right arm caressingly round his neck. ' "I'll cheer you up, my pious little boy. But are you really going to let me sit on your knee, darling? You won't be angry? Say the word and I'll get off." ' But suddenly she discovers that his beloved guru, Father Zossima, is dead. Her mood changes totally: ' "So, Father Zossima's dead!" cried Grushenka. "Good gracious! and I didn't know!" She crossed herself devoutly. "Goodness, what have I been doing? Sitting on his knee like that now!" She started as though in dismay, jumped off Aloysha's knee at once and sat down on the sofa.'

And Aloysha responds in the manner of a saint. He says in a loud voice to the man who has brought him into this supposed den of vice: ' "You'd better take an example from her: did you see how she took pity on me? I came here thinking to find a wicked soul – I felt drawn to wickedness because I was mean and wicked myself, but I've found a true sister. I've found a treasure – a loving soul. She took pity on me just now ... I'm talking about you, Grushenka. You've just restored my soul." '

The fallen woman is won over instantaneously. ' "I'm going to cry, I am! I am! He called me his sister and I shall never forget it, never!" '

Total forgetfulness of self and absolute forgiveness are features of Dostoevsky's saint; so is unlimited warmth of love.

T. S. Eliot

T. S. Eliot, who became a devout Anglican, will reveal some similarities with Evelyn Waugh, who became a devout Roman

Catholic. Both of them had a strong underlying awareness of the will of God for each one of us. One might attempt to find some analogy between Dostoevksy's Idiot and one or more of Graham Greene's fallible heroes. But the attempt breaks down. There was nothing morally fallible about the Idiot, Father Zossima or Aloysha.

Eliot, Professor Cunningham has argued, 'sees the Incarnation as the supreme moment when the fragility of time intersects with the infinite'. Only the saint has a continuous sense of the presence of the infinite in the midst of the passage of time in life.

> to apprehend
> The point of intersection of the timeless
> With time, is an occupation for the saint –
> No occupation either, but something given
> And taken, in a lifetime's death in love,
> Ardour and selflessness and self surrender.
> For most of us, there is only the unattended
> Moment, the moment in and out of time.
>
> ('Dry Salvages' in *Four Quartets*)

For our purposes, it is more useful to concentrate on possible saints, actual or fictitious, in, for example, *Murder in the Cathedral* and *The Cocktail Party*.

Thomas à Becket was born in 1118 and in 1170 was murdered by officers of King Henry II. Henry had asked himself the question, aloud: 'Who will rid me of this turbulent priest?', but is generally acquitted of the intention to murder Thomas. In 1155, Becket became Chancellor and a bosom friend of Henry's. He subordinated during this period the interests of the Church, of which he was an Archdeacon by this time, to those of his royal master. In 1162, he became Archbishop of Canterbury, though still at the time a simple Deacon. Before a year had passed, he was on the worst of terms with the King, having by now become a bold advocate of the claims of the Church.

In November 1164 Becket fled to France. Six years later, after some kind of reconciliation had taken place between the Pope and Henry, Thomas returned to England, with no intention whatsoever of yielding to Henry's claims. The Pope was prevailed upon to suspend the bishops who had favoured Henry's cause. Becket was murdered by what are now called over-zealous courtiers of Henry.

He was canonised within two years. His shrine was plundered by Henry VIII, to whom the memory of Becket was especially obnoxious.

What is unique in T. S. Eliot's *Murder in the Cathedral* is the unflinching way in which the temptations attendant on martyrdom and possible sanctity are presented. Thomas, we quickly learn, is not devoid of arrogance. As soon as he appears it is evident that he has set his heart on a glorious termination:

> Neither does the agent suffer
> Nor the patient act. But both are fixed
> In an eternal action, an eternal patience
> To which all must consent that it may be willed
> And which all must suffer that they may will it,
> That the pattern may subsist, for the pattern is the action
> And the suffering, that the wheel may turn and still
> Be forever still.

But when the Tempter says: 'Your Lordship is too proud', he seems to have a point. When some kind of deal is offered him, he haughtily answers:

> No! shall I, who keep the keys
> Of heaven and hell, supreme alone in England,
> Who bind and loose, with power from the Pope,
> Descend to desire a punier power?
> Delegate to deal the doom of damnation,
> To condemn kings, not serve among their servants,
> Is my open office. No! Go.

He rises above such attitudes, but a more profound spiritual temptation is offered him. The Tempter plays on what he imagines is his greatest weakness. He lays out before him 'a vision of eternal grandeur'. Thomas is well aware of the danger and does not overcome it easily:

> Is there no way, in my soul's sickness,
> Does not lead to damnation in pride?
> I well know that these temptations
> Mean present vanity and future torment.
> Can sinful pride be driven out
> Only by more sinful? Can I neither act nor suffer
> Without perdition?

Eliot seems to be telling us that as long as the dilemma is approached in merely human terms, it is insoluble. One must move away from oneself and seek above all else the will of God. St Thomas in the play is represented as delivering a sermon shortly before his murder, which he foresees all too clearly. He discusses at some length the right way to think of a martyr and insists that a Christian martyrdom is never an accident. Saints are not made by accident. 'Still less is a Christian martyrdom the effect of a man's will to become a saint, as a man by willing and contriving may become a ruler of men. A martyrdom is always the design of God, for His love of men, to warn them and to lead them, to bring them back to His ways. It is never the design of man; for the true martyr is he who has become the instrument of God, who has lost his will in the will of God, and who no longer desires anything for himself, not even the glory of martyrdom.'

When the murderous moment approaches, Thomas's acolytes want him to 'bar the doors', but he has no doubts about the will of God by this time. 'We have fought the beast and have conquered; we have only to conquer now by suffering. This is the easier victory. Now is the triumph of the Cross, now open the door! I command it. Open the door!'

And the door was duly opened to martyrdom and sanctity.

Anyone who was told that a saint would emerge from T. S. Eliot's 'comedy' *The Cocktail Party*, would have to wait some time, as in a detective story, and probably make a few wrong guesses. It turns out in the end to be Celia Coplestone, a woman of uncertain age who is earlier involved in some kind of illicit romance with Edward Chamberlain, but who at the end rises above the others in undisputed integrity. A mysterious figure later identified as Sir Henry Harcourt-Reilly, half psychiatrist, half spiritual guru, points out to her a terrible line of duty. Celia confesses that she suffers from a peculiar kind of spiritual disability: 'In fact I think it would really be dishonest for me, now, to try to make a life with *any*body! I couldn't give anyone the kind of love – I wish I could – which belongs to that life. Oh, I'm afraid this sounds like raving! Or just cantankerousness . . . still, if there's no other way . . . then I feel just hopeless.'

Reilly replies: 'There *is* another way, if you have the courage. . . . You will journey blind, but the way leads towards possession of what you have sought for in the wrong place.' She places herself in his hands and we hear, in the third act two years later, of the outcome; Celia is dead. She had joined an order, a very austere one, and as she had already had experience of nursing:

> She was directed to Kinkanja,
> Where there are various endemic diseases
> Besides, of course, those brought by Europeans,
> And where the conditions are favourable to plague.

An insurrection broke out.

When everyone else fled, Celia Coplestone remained. She was taken:

> When our people got there, they questioned the villagers –
> Those who survived. And then they found her body,
> Or at least they found traces of it.

She had in fact been crucified: 'very near an anthill'. Later it seems the natives erected 'a sort of shrine to Celia and propitiated her with offerings of fruit and flowers, fowls and sucking-pigs'.

The plain man in the play, Edward, expressed the hope that she had not suffered as ordinary people suffer. Reilly replies

> Not at all what I mean, Rather the contrary.
> I'd say that she suffered all that we should suffer
> In fear and pain and loathing – all these together –
> And reluctance of the body to become a *thing*.
> I'd say she suffered more, because more conscious
> Than the rest of us. She paid the highest price
> In suffering. That is part of the design.

Total commitment to and conformity with the 'pattern' or the 'design'. We come across the same idea in Evelyn Waugh's conception of sanctity.

Graham Greene and Evelyn Waugh

Graham Greene and Evelyn Waugh are generally agreed to be the two greatest Catholic novelists writing in the English language in the present century. I have known Graham Greene slightly; Evelyn Waugh, who died in 1966, I knew very well. He had much to do with my conversion to Catholicism. I am proud to be a godfather of his eldest son. We shared an enormous religious debt to Father Martin d'Arcy, SJ.

Malcolm Muggeridge, an old friend of Graham Greene, who came to admire Evelyn Waugh in later years, said of them: 'Graham is a saint trying to be a sinner; Evelyn was a sinner trying to be a saint.' I should prefer to say that Graham Greene found it easier to love the sinner; Evelyn to hate the sin.

These two superb writers, Greene the supreme story-teller, Waugh the master of English prose, were born in 1904 and 1903 respectively, both educated at English public schools and Oxford, both of them Catholic converts. It would be natural to expect some similarities in their approach to sanctity. A certain heroic quality has strongly appealed to them both. But for me the contrasts are as striking as the likenesses.

Evelyn Waugh after his conversion was a strictly orthodox Catholic in his life and thought. Graham Greene has never presented himself in such a light. That has not prevented him from being a favourite author of many strict and ardent Catholics. His affection for the Church, in spite of all his reservations, does not seem to have wavered. *The Power and the Glory* (1940) was dedicated to Father Gervase Mathew, *Monsignor Quixote* (1982) to another priest and Tom Burns, editor of *The Tablet*. Thoughtful Catholics have always felt that Greene presented a side of Catholicism which was apt to be overlooked in official teaching, but was close to the spirit of Jesus. They have in mind his tenderness towards sinners. Greene is almost fanatically tolerant. He wrote an introduction to Kim Philby's *Memoirs* (Philby was a war-time friend) in which he concluded: 'I take off my hat to Kim Philby.' One does not associate Evelyn Waugh with such a condonation of treachery.

Greene has written over thirty books. For me and for many others, the best will always be *The Power and the Glory*. Sir Hugh Walpole wrote of it: 'A most remarkable novel; Mr Greene proves by it that he is the finest English novelist of his generation.' The hero is a 'whisky priest' who insists on staying at his post and performing his priestly duties during a religious persecution in Mexico when he has more than one opportunity to escape. He has fathered an illegitimate child. According to the ordinary rules of Christianity he is not a good man, though always capable of showing kindness. He is caught and executed. 'After the long night of waiting for the coming dawn the priest, bolstered somewhat by a gift of brandy from the lieutenant, went unsteadily and fearfully to his execution with an interior sense of abandonment' (*The Meaning of Saints* by Lawrence Cunningham).

A memorable aftermath is described in the book. A pious mother is reading to her rather bored son about past martyrs. Suddenly he asks her: ' "And that one," the boy said, "they shot today. Was he a hero too?"

"Yes."

"The one who stayed with us that time?"

"Yes. He was one of the martyrs of the Church."

"He had a funny smell," one of the little girls said.

"You must never say that again," the mother said. "He may be one of the saints."

"Shall we pray to him then?"

The mother hesitated. "It would do no harm. Of course, before we *know* he is a saint, there will have to be miracles. . . ."

"Did he call out " 'Viva el Cristo Rey?' " the boy asked.

"Yes. He was one of the heroes of the faith." '

Greene's fictitious hero undoubtedly owes something to an actual fugitive priest who died a martyr's death in Mexico thirteen years before Greene's book appeared. Father Miguel Pro Juarez, SJ, returned clandestinely to Mexico in 1926 and carried on a surreptitious ministry until 1927, when he was captured and executed. What is interesting here is that Evelyn Waugh, in his *Life of Edmund Campion SJ*, (1935) makes an explicit comparison with the same Mexican priest, Padre Pro.

Edmund Campion, initially a brilliant star in the world of Oxford and the darling of Queen Elizabeth's favourite, Leicester, found it necessary to escape to France in 1570. Years later, by now a Jesuit priest and an intellectual of European fame, he returned secretly to England, as part of a mission which must eventually lead to his arrest and execution. The purpose of the mission was avowedly religious and non-political, but in those days the distinction was not likely to save the missioners.

After moving about the country for several months spent in inspiring the faithful, Campion was caught in a priest-hole like a rat in a trap. In a personal encounter with Queen Elizabeth and Leicester he was offered preferment if he would renege. There was of course no question of that. After he was found guilty, his final words were: 'It was not our death that ever we feared. But we knew that we were not lords of our own lives and therefore for want of an answer would not be guilty of our deaths. The only thing that we have now to say is, that if our religion do make us traitors, we are worthy to be condemned; but otherwise are, and have been, good subjects as ever the Queen had.'

He went on to insist that what was now being qualified 'with the odious name of treason' had been thought 'by all the ancient priests, bishops and kings'. His voice rose in triumph: 'God lives; posterity will live; their judgment is not so liable to corruption as that of those who are now going to sentence us to death.'

The Lord Chief Justice brutally replied in the fashion then approved of: 'You must go to the place from whence you came, there to remain until ye shall be drawn through the open City of London upon hurdles to the place of execution, and there be hanged and let down alive, and your privy parts cut off, and your entrails taken out and burnt in your sight; then your head be cut off and your body divided into four parts, to be disposed of at her Majesty's pleasure, And God have mercy on your soul.' In the event Campion was spared none of these barbarities.

The external contrast between the behaviour of the fictitious priest and the real one is sharp enough. No one is likely to deny the title of martyr to either of them. In each case, a spiritual factor is laid before us. Greene puts into the mind of his whisky priest a few final reflections. ' "What an impossible fellow I am," he thought, "and how useless." He felt only an immense disappointment because he had to go to God empty-handed, with nothing done at all. It seemed to him, at that moment, that it would have been quite easy to have been a saint. It would only have needed a little self-restraint and a little courage. He felt like someone who has missed happiness by seconds at an appointed place. He knew now that at the end there was only one thing that counted – to be a saint.'

Evelyn Waugh points to a spiritual moral in different terms. 'Campion stands out from even his most gallant and chivalrous contemporaries by the supernatural grace that was in him.' The gentle scholar was able to step straight into a world of violence and acquit himself nobly. The man capable of the strenuous heroism of the last year and a half was able without any complaint to pursue the humdrum routine of the pedagogue and contemplate without hesitation a lifetime so employed. Waugh finds here a mystery

which 'sets Campion's triumph apart from the ordinary achievements of human strength; a mystery whose solution lies in the
busy, uneventful years at Brunn and Prague, in the profound and
accurate piety of the Jesuit rule.'

Martyrs indubitably, but saints? Campion was not canonised
until 1970 after Waugh wrote his book. If we are looking for
Christ-like qualities, it is worth noting the forgiveness that both
extended, not without difficulty, to the men who had betrayed
them. The half-caste approaches the whisky priest, after the
latter's arrest.

> 'You are a good man, Father, but you think the worst of people. I
> just want your blessing, that's all.'
> 'What is the good? You can't sell a blessing,' the priest said.
> 'It's just because we won't see each other again. And I didn't want
> you to go off there thinking ill things. . . .'
> 'You are so superstitious,' the priest said. 'You think my blessing
> will be like a blinker over God's eyes. I can't stop him knowing all
> about it. Much better go home and pray. Then if He gives you grace to
> feel sorry, give away the money. . . .'
> 'What money, Father?' The half-caste shook his stirrup angrily.
> 'What money?'
> 'There you go again. . . .' The priest did his best, but could only
> manage 'I'll pray for you' before he rode off.

He was human enough to have 'at least one cause for satisfaction –
that yellow and unreliable faith would be absent at the death'.

Campion was able to be rather more forthcoming. The spy who
visited him in prison insisted: ' "If I had thought that you would
have had to suffer aught but imprisonment through my accusing
of you, I would never have done it," he said. "However, I might
have lost by it." "If that is the case," replied Campion, "I beseech
you, in God's name, to do penance, and confess your crime, to
God's glory and your own salvation." But the spy was really
concerned to save himself from the possible vengeance of the
Catholics. "To make you quite safe," said Campion, "I will if you
please recommend you to a Catholic duke in Germany, where you
may live in perfect security." '

From all we read, Campion was such a blameless character that
his claim to be a saint in the light of his martyrdom seems
irresistible. But as for the whisky priest in *The Power and the Glory*, it

is hardly conceivable that he would be judged a saint by even the most liberal tribunal. Saint Augustine and many other saints led sinful lives, but in due course they repented. It does not seem that conscious repentance is credited to Greene's hero. Yet he continues to appeal to vast numbers who would find less to attract them in the more orthodox Catholic. Certainly his sense of guilt is very endearing, and goes with a humility which has always been attributed to saints. Like a number of them, he considered himself to be the first of sinners.

But to understand Greene's devotion to this fallen priest, one may take a look at another of his books, *Don Quixote*. Don Quixote is not, I think, presented to us as a saint, but he is a lovable character. In taking leave of his somewhat shrewish housekeeper, he assures her: ' "For a Christian, there is no such thing as goodbye for ever." But he qualified this statement to himself. "I believed what I told her, I believed it, of course, but how is it that when I speak of belief I become aware always of a shadow of disbelief haunting my belief?" ' 'The shadow of disbelief haunting my belief', there Graham Greene seems to sum up a deep aspect of his own religion and to appeal to countless men and women who share his problem.

Evelyn Waugh exposed himself in one of his books more thoroughly than Graham Greene has ever done. In *The Ordeal of Gilbert Pinfold* he described a nervous breakdown with clinical accuracy; but for him, any failure to believe was a kind of weakness. With Greene, it has remained a sympathetic quality.

Greene has rightly been described as a very compassionate writer. In one of his books, Scobie, the police officer, confesses to himself: 'It isn't beauty that we love, it's failure. Beauty is like success, we can't love it for long.' And moral failure, as long as there is still some residue of resistance, has a special charm for Greene. His doctrine is not quite that attributed to Rasputin – 'sin for salvation' – but at times it comes close to it.

It will help us to understand Evelyn Waugh's approach to sanctity if we glance at his *Life of St Helena*, the dowager Empress of Constantine the Great, who was canonised because of her discovery of the True Cross. Evelyn Waugh wrote what he calls a 'novel' about her, and also an essay in a collection of personal studies edited by Philip Caraman, SJ. In extreme old age, Helena, who may have been born in Britain, made a journey to Jerusalem, and discovered there the relics of the True Cross now venerated everywhere in Christendom. 'Numberless churches are dedicated to her; numberless girls baptised with her name; she appears everywhere in painting, sculpture and mosaic. She has fitted in a homely and substantial way into the family life of Christendom.' Evelyn Waugh summarises her achievement and, in doing so, reveals his own strongest convictions about the nature of sanctity: 'Her work was finished. She had done what only the saints succeeded in doing, what indeed constitutes their pattern of sanctity. She had completely conformed to the will of God. Others a few years back had done their duty gloriously in the arena. Hers was a gentler task, merely to gather wood. That was the particular humble task for which she had been created.' The last expression is repeated by Evelyn Waugh at the end of the essay mentioned above. 'What we can learn from Helena is something about the workings of God: that He wants a different thing from each of us, laborious or easy, conspicuous or quite private. But something which only we can do and for which we were each created.'

Can we imagine Graham Greene and Evelyn Waugh being asked to join forces in pronouncing on the claims of candidates for canonisation? It is difficult to picture them agreeing on anything except the fact of martyrdom. But possibly we can say that the first qualities they would both look for would be purity of intention and an indomitable search for God.

23
CONCLUSION

H. A. Fisher, author of the classic *History of Europe* wrote a shade ironically that other men wiser and more learned than himself had found in human history a systematic pattern, a coherent design. His own prevailing impression was of the contingent and the unforeseen. It may be that men wiser and more learned than myself would claim to be able to pin down the nature of saintliness, to draw the composite portrait of a saint. If so, as far as I am aware, they have failed to do so hitherto; I shall not presume to attempt success where they have failed.

Father Philip Caraman, SJ, has edited several books about the saints. He has contributed an authoritative essay, from the Roman Catholic point of view, to an important study of holiness. He is reluctant to embark on generalisations. In a book called *Saints and Ourselves* in which twelve saints are selected for discussion Philip Caraman, as editor, wrote: 'I recall the lines of Gerald Manley Hopkins, who wrote of the diversity of sanctity in one of his sonnets: "Christ," he said, "prays in ten thousand places, lovely in limbs and lovely in eyes not his, to the Father through the features of men's faces." ' He adds this verdict: 'No saint is like any other, and none is wholly imitable, though all offer some light to guide us in the twilight of this life.' There is not much to console the seeker after generalisations there.

In this book I have discussed eighteen selected saints canonised by the Catholic Church and two Orthodox saints. The total number of canonised saints is uncertain but it runs to several thousand. It would be generally agreed that many times that number of men and women have deserved the label. To produce a composite portrait of this vast assembly would be rather ridiculous. To produce one of our eighteen selected Catholic saints is not much easier. Who can honestly establish an identity between, for example, Saint Peter, Saint Augustine, Saint Joan of Arc, Saint Thomas More, Saint John of the Cross and Saint Teresa of Lisieux?

In a moment I will point to a number of characteristics common to all or most of the eighteen. But still the special nature of sanctity is likely to elude us, as it surely would if we were undertaking a study of artistic genius or statesmanship.

As a Roman Catholic I find it easy to believe that the Holy Spirit has been at work in the process of canonisation. Non-Catholics are of course at liberty to accept or reject that assumption, but I do not underestimate the element of human choice in the selection process. Hitherto the Catholic Church has only canonised Catholics. With the splendid development of ecumenicism in recent years I entertain high hopes that in time to come the net will be cast more widely, the meaning of sanctity may be freshly interpreted.

The Orthodox Church canonises saints in its own fashion. I have discussed two of them here. I have added three outstanding servants of God. One of them, Cardinal Newman, is quite likely to be canonised one day. The other two, Martin Luther and Archbishop Temple, must rank among the religious giants. Many of those commemorated in the Anglican prayer book, including such non-Anglicans as John Wesley and John Bunyan, have exhibited many of the qualities attributed to the canonised saints. But it would need a different book to work out such comparisons. I have less compunction in omitting leading representatives of other religions such as Mohamed, Buddha, Gandhi and Maimonides, though the Jews to whom Christianity is enormously indebted, raise a special issue. Those just mentioned lacked one overwhelming characteristic of the canonised saints, a total commitment to, and love of, Jesus Christ. *A fortiori* there can be no place here for noble-minded humanists from Socrates to Thomas Huxley.

Against the above background I study briefly below three attempts that have been made to analyse sanctity which deserve our attention. The most thorough examination of sanctity by a writer of fame and insight is that by William James, the illustrious American psychologist. His Gifford lectures (1901–2), published as *The Varieties of Religious Experience*, contain over sixty pages on saintliness and more than forty-five on 'The Value of Saintliness'.

James was a deeply religious man but a very unorthodox Christian, if he could be called a Christian at all. His taste was certainly catholic but with a small c. In the course of his lectures he refers to 'the greatest saints, the spritual heroes whom everyone acknowledges.' 'The saintly character,' he says, 'is the character for which spiritual emotions are the habitual centre of the personal energy: and there is a certain composite photograph of universal saintliness, the same in all religions, of which the features can all be traced.' The features he selects are these:

(1) A feeling of being in a wider life than that of this world's selfish little interests and the conviction, not merely intellectual but as it were sensible, of the existence of an ideal power. In Christian saintliness, this power is always personified as God.
(2) A sense of the 'friendly' continuity of the ideal power with our own life, and a willing self-surrender to its control.
(3) An immense elation and freedom, as the outlines of the confining selfhood melt down.
(4) A shifting of the emotional centre towards loving and harmonious affections, towards 'yes' and away from 'no', where the claims of the non-ego are concerned.

These 'fundamental inner conditions,' James says, 'have characteristic practical consequences: (a) asceticism; (b) strength of soul; (c) purity; (d) charity.'

In his lecture on 'The Value of Saintliness', he dwells at length on the excesses that can result from an unbalanced saintliness – the crazier kinds of self-mortification. He comes down, however, on the side of social benefits which have been conferred by the saints on humanity. 'They are impregnators of the world, vivifiers and animators of potentialities of goodness which, but for them, would live for ever dormant. It is not possible to be quite as mean as we naturally are, when they have passed before us.'

Professor Cunningham, Professor of Religion at Florida State University, has produced a book, *The Meaning of Saints*, which in a cool, academic way is invaluable. 'A saint,' says Cunningham, 'is a person so grasped by a religious vision that it becomes central to his or her life in a way that radically changes the person and leads others to glimpse the value of that vision.' Cunningham considers that sanctity begins in a conversion: it does not occur at the precise moment of that conversion. What gives the saint credibility as a saint is the sustained unfolding of his or her life in contact with the ordinary demands of reality. What strikes one about a Dietrich Bonhoeffer is not that he died at the hands of the Gestapo, but that he reflected, prayed, wrote, counselled and lived under the

extreme circumstances of a Gestapo regime. His thoughts and
ideas take on a compelling significance simply because he worked
them out under conditions where lesser persons would have been
preoccupied with problems of personal survival. Bonhoeffer is one
of Cunningham's saints. He is not one of mine, but he was a fine
man and indubitably a martyr. Can a saint be actively associated
with an assassination plot?

Cunningham has not much time for miracles, prayers granted
by the saints, or for 'veneration'. He insists none the less that the
saint is still a figure of much significance. 'What should concern
us,' he says, 'is the side of the saint which emphasises the
prophetic, the exemplary, the moral dimension', and what he calls
'the challenge'. Cunningham acknowledges, however, that 'it is
unlikely that the intercessory elements of Christian piety will go
away; they are too deeply rooted in the common religious
experience of humanity'.

Canon Douillet is pleasantly dogmatic. His book *What is a Saint?*
contains a chapter entitled 'The Spirit of the Saints' in which he
picks out eight common characteristics: (1) faith; (2) courage to
choose; (3) unified love; (4) genius; (5) heroism; (6) asceticism
and holiness; (7) prayer; (8) miracles.

I will take these in my own order. I cannot agree that genius in
any ordinary sense is a distinguishing quality of a saint. It can be
reasonably attributed to not a few of our selected eighteen – Saint
Augustine, Saint Teresa of Avila, Saint John of the Cross, Saint
Francis de Sale among them. But it would be totally inappropriate
to use the term in connection with the vast majority of those who
have been canonised. Miracles raise a more thorny question. In
this matter I must be regarded as a minimiser. I do not dispute the
fact of the miracles accepted by the Catholic Church, but as
brought out earlier in a quotation from Father Caraman, they are
certainly not regarded as a prerequisite of canonisation in the
twentieth century. I surmise that their significance will grow
increasingly less, and I shall not be sorry.

May be I am a little biased here. My great-uncle, who began life
as the Honourable Charles Reginald Pakenham, nephew of the
Duke of Wellington, and became a Grenadier officer, finished up
as a Passionist monk who took that Order to Dublin. Walking
barefoot about the streets and living among the poor a life of
poverty, he was regarded as a saint. When he died the cry went up

throughout the Dublin slums 'The saint is dead.' A hundred and twenty years have passed since then. No miracles have been attributed to him, nor has he even been beatified, but I would not personally be able to think of him as more holy if miracles had been claimed on his behalf.

I do not believe that 'if miracles go, saints will go with them.' That would be an unduly iconoclastic thought. The Catholic Church will surely develop its views on sanctity as it has developed them on so many other things.

Faith presents a much simpler issue. The saints had a much stronger faith than most of us. Real saints have believed wholly and completely in the invisible realities of their Credo. When the saints said they believed in everlasting life they were not repeating a formula; their whole existence was given up to that certainty. That does not mean that they have been immune from temptations against faith. I have mentioned earlier the terrible feeling of anguish which Saint Teresa of Lisieux endured throughout the last eighteen months of her life. 'I was lost in darkness from out of which came an accursed voice: "Are you sure God loves you? Has he come to tell you so Himself?"' Saint Francis de Sales tells us that Saint Francis of Assisi was plagued by similar temptations for two whole years. Christ asked Saint Peter when he thought he was drowning, 'O you of little faith! Why did you doubt?' The Catholic Church was, in human terms, founded on a man who knew all there was to know about the difficulty of maintaining faith.

Courage to choose and heroism run into one another as do the physical and moral forms of courage. Saints generally have rejected half-measures and compromises because they have loved God so intensely. The obvious case is that of the martyrs. They had to make a clear choice – either Christ and death or life to be achieved by disowning Him. Among the saints dealt with here Saint Ignatius of Antioch, Saint Polycarp, Saints Perpetua and Felicity, Saint Thomas More and Saint Maximilian Kolbe chose Christ and sacrificed life, others dramatically accepted conversion. Of these, never forgetting Saint Paul, the most famous is Saint Augustine. How far grace determined their decision and how far it was entirely a free act raises questions too profound to be gone into here. Heroism is plain enough in the case of the martyrs and, if one looks below the surface, in the case of all the saints. But heroism, even heroic virtue, is not confined to saints or religious believers.

Asceticism and holiness we certainly associate with saints. Sometimes as with Saint Simeon Stylites who spent thirty years on the top of a pillar we feel that they carried it to excess. But the most joyful saints can be the most mortified, Saint Francis of Assisi being a striking example. No one who was not in some sense ascetic would be acceptable as a saint. There have been fat saints such as Saint Thomas Aquinas but one prefers a saint to look like Cardinal Newman. No saint has failed to join his or her sufferings with those of Christ.

All saints are men and women of prayer. Some are primarily contemplative, others involved in charitable works and evangelism. Saint Teresa of Avila and Saint Ignatius of Loyola are classic examples of both ways of serving God. But the same in greater or lesser degree could be said of all our eighteen. Saint Joan of Arc, however, who died when she was nineteen is not easily thought of as a contemplative, nor did Saint Teresa of Lisieux who died at twenty-four have wide opportunities of doing good works.

By 'unified love' Canon Douillet means that the saints' love for God does not prevent them from loving all around them, but their love of their fellow men is permeated by their love of God. Saint Francis's fondness for his brethren and Saint Teresa of Avila's for her nuns are among the best-known examples.

We have now considered the attempts of a psychologist, a professor of religion and a Catholic priest to define the qualities inherent in a saint. My own analysis provides rather different headings. In the widest terms the saints have exhibited three main characteristics: they have believed implicitly that they have received a message from God; they have made a lasting impression by what they did; and an impression no less lasting by what they were.

There would be no general agreement as to which of the eighteen saints discussed in this book could fairly be described as mystics. Mysticism has been defined in various ways, as mentioned earlier. A sense of direct contact with God is a minimum requirement; some would claim that there must be awareness of Divine union. In a standard book on mysticism by F. P. Happold already mentioned, out of thirty men and women listed only three of mine are included – Saint Augustine, Saint Teresa of Avila, and Saint John of the Cross. . . . But this is surely much too restrictive. Saint Catherine of Siena must be reckoned a mystic by any standard and there are others among our selection who have powerful claims. Most, if not all, of our eighteen received what they believed were direct communications from God.

I will quote a number of examples. St Peter is in a different position from the others, having received a direct mandate from Jesus Christ: 'Thou art Peter and upon this rock I will build my church – Feed my sheep – follow thou Me.' St Perpetua, before her struggles with the beasts in the arena, dreamed that she fought with a huge and ugly Egyptian. She overcame him and received a branch with golden apples. The bearer of it kissed her, saying: 'Peace be with you, daughter.' 'And I awoke, understanding that I should not fight with beasts but with the Devil. But I knew that victory was mine.'

St Patrick 'saw in the night visions a man whose name was Victorious coming as it were from Ireland with countless letters. . . . He heard voices crying as with one mouth: "We beseech thee, holy youth, to come and walk among us once more." '

St Augustine could be quoted at great length, but this passage must suffice: 'Too late I loved Thee, O Thou Beauty of ancient days, yet ever new! Too late I loved Thee, and behold Thou wert within and I abroad, and there I searched for Thee . . . Thou calledst, and shoutedst, and burstedst my deafness . . . Thou flashedst, shonedst, and scatteredst my blindness. Thou breathedst odours and I drew in breath and pant for Thee. I tasted, and hunger and thirst. Thou touchedst me, and I burn for Thy peace.'

St Catherine of Siena received a long series of messages in her dialogue with God, culminating in this one: 'Truth is founded on the living rock, the gentle Christ Jesus clothed in a light that can discern darkness. Clothe yourself in this light, dearest daughter, whom I so love in truth.'

St Francis had a number of visions, far more, probably, than have been recorded. What is sometimes called 'the third stroke' was decisive. 'As he was passing the church of St Damian which was "threatening to collapse with age" (Bonaventure), he felt the urge to go in and pray. As he knelt in prayer before the image of Christ crucified, all of a sudden he heard a voice coming from the Cross and telling him three times: "Francis, go and repair my house, for you see that it is all falling down." He rose to his feet in an ecstasy of joy.'

St Joan of Arc's voices are familiar to us all. 'I was in my thirteenth year,' she said at the trial, 'when God sent a voice to guide me. At first I was very frightened. The voice came towards the hour of noon, in summer, in my father's garden. I had fasted the previous day. I heard the voice on my right hand, in the direction of the church. I seldom hear it without [seeing] a light. That light always appears on the side from which I hear the voice.'

St Ignatius of Loyola abandoned his life as a soldier and young gallant to live as a ragged mendicant. On the banks of the river Cardona he underwent a spiritual experience which inspired him for the rest of his life and gave him the strength and imagination to found the Society of Jesus. His mind was so illuminated (see page 85) that he seemed to himself to have become another man and to possess a quite different understanding.

St Teresa of Avila underwent as many spiritual experiences as anyone, it would seem, that ever lived. To quote her own words: 'These ecstasies come upon me with great violence and in such a way as to be outwardly visible, I having no power to resist them even when I am with others, for they come in such a way as to admit of no disguising them unless it be by letting people suppose that, as I am subject to disease of the heart, they are fainting fits. I take great pains to resist them when they are coming on – sometimes I cannot do it.'

St John of the Cross underwent mystical experiences which we can only understand faintly, if at all. One stanza of the *Living Flame of Love* epitomises the flavour:

O living flame of love
That tenderly wounds my soul
In its deepest centre! Since
Now You are not oppressive,
Now consummate! if it be your will:
Tear through the veil of this sweet encounter!

St Teresa of Lisieux accepted and rejoiced in suffering in a manner few of us can understand; yet no one can doubt that it was linked to her sanctity.

I have quoted from eleven of our eighteen selected saints. I am not suggesting that the direct religious experience of the others was necessarily weaker.

What then of the achievement? We have already mentioned the martyrs whose example has persisted through the ages. Great religious orders were founded by, or in memory of, not a few saints; St Augustine, St Francis of Assisi, St Ignatius of Loyola, St Teresa of Avila, St Vincent de Paul, St Francis de Sales. The Christian church in Ireland was effectively established by St Patrick. St Peter was the first Pope.

No general historian ignores the influence of St Peter, St Augustine, St Patrick, St Catherine of Siena, St Joan of Arc, St Thomas More, St Ignatius of Loyola, St Vincent de Paul and others.

Several of our selected saints have written spiritual classics. St Augustine, St Catherine of Siena, St John of the Cross, St Francis de Sales, St Teresa of Lisieux come readily to mind while most of the others have left writings of much religious value. The authors, however, of some of the best-known spiritual books have not been canonised. For many years I used to refer to 'Saint' Thomas à Kempis until I learnt my mistake. Yet other men and women not recognised as saints have had a conviction of divine inspiration and affected world history in that conviction; Oliver Cromwell for example. No one today refers to Oliver Cromwell as 'Saint' Oliver.

It may be said that saints exhibit heroic virtue and this has been a requirement for canonisation by the Catholic Church. I would happily apply this phrase to someone like Clement Attlee, the most selfless and quietly heroic figure that I have encountered in public life. I have never met a layman of higher ethical standards. But when Attlee was asked if he was a Christian he replied: 'Accept the Christian ethic, can't stand the mumbo jumbo.' Christian sanctity if it is to have any meaning at all implies a loving relationship with God and with Christ.

William James, the dispassionate psychologist, considered it would have been extraordinary if those who loved God so intensely and were ready to subdue self so totally had not reflected that love and discipline in their attitude to their fellow men. And the expected has happened. But in addition to their distinctive virtue the saints have indubitably possessed an aura all their own.

But it is no part of my purpose to present the saints as perfect, although I would not wish to discourage those who have gained strength from that conviction. The ethical perfection of the saints is not, in my understanding, an article of faith in any Church.

St Thomas More is almost certainly the most revered of English saints, but his attitude to heretics is repulsive by our modern standards. St Peter fell and fell again. Almost at the end of his life he appears to have been seeking to avoid his destiny. St Augustine's sins before he became a Christian add to the drama of his conversion. But the dismissal of his mistress, the mother of his child, seems harsh to us, though not apparently to him. St Francis of Assisi's treatment of his father makes painful reading. And there are numerous other examples.

Nevertheless the saints have, speaking generally, been recognised as such – in their lifetime, widely if not universally.

If I am asked to illustrate what I mean by an aura, I would turn first to someone who is not yet canonized – Cardinal Newman, (see page 156 above). In 1882, The Lord Chief Justice of England Lord Coleridge, tried to explain what he felt in Newman's presence: 'I cannot analyse it or explain it, but to this hour he interests and awes me like no other man I ever saw. He is as simple and humble and playful as a child and yet I am with a being unlike anyone else. He lifts me up for a time and subdues me – if I said frightens me it would hardly be too strong; and if he does this to a commonplace old lawyer, what must he be to men who can really enter into him and feel with him!'

So it was, each in their own fashion, with the others. I give three illustrations here: the spiritual adviser of St Catherine of Siena, Raymond of Capua, wrote: 'Being so closely associated with her, I was able to see at first hand how, as soon as she was freed from the occupations in which she was engaged for the work of souls, at once, one might almost say by a natural process, her mind was raised to the things of heaven.'

We are told (page 89) that the year before he died, Ignatius (of Loyola) behaved with great harshness to Lainez who was to succeed him. Lainez felt so badly that he had recourse to the Lord and said: 'Lord, what have I done against our Society that this saint treats me in this fashion?'

Saint Teresa of Avila said of St John of the Cross: 'They take him for a saint, and a saint in my opinion he is and has been all his life.'

Can this indescribable aura be linked to any one virtue? 'Blessed are the pure in heart' we are told in the Sermon on the Mount, 'for they shall see God.' The saints we can be sure are seeing God now. But if only through a glass darkly, they saw Him here below, and down the years have helped millions of men, women and children to see Him also.

The future of sanctity as interpreted by the Roman Catholic Church is wrapped in obscurity, although I believe that as the years pass its spiritual significance will not diminish. I feel sure myself that miracles will figure less and less prominently.

Most people, of all religions and none, are ready to agree that Mother Theresa of Calcutta is bound to be canonised in due course. No doubt she will be. My revered friend Malcolm Muggeridge interprets as miraculous a sun lighting up when he was televising her in semi-darkness. Whether or not he is right there, it does not seem to me to affect the question of her sanctity which has long been evident to all who meet her.

Modern communications enable the whole world to learn much more quickly than of old about heroic deeds. But canonisation has never been confined to famous figures and never will be. One crucial decision before the Catholic Church will be whether to extend the range of its saints beyond its own membership. I hope and believe that this will begin to happen before too many years have passed.

The precise requirements demanded by the Catholic Church are certain to vary from time to time. Their selection, with infinite care, of a limited number of men and women in whom the Divine Spirit is deemed to have been at work will never fail to provide an enormous encouragement to all who look for spiritual help from that same spirit.

INDEX